DISRUPTION IN THE BOARDROOM

LEADING CORPORATE GOVERNANCE AND OVERSIGHT INTO AN EVOLVING DIGITAL FUTURE

Jennifer C. Wolfe

Disruption in the Boardroom: Leading Corporate Governance and Oversight into an Evolving Digital Future

Jennifer C. Wolfe
Bluffton, SC, USA

ISBN-13 (pbk): 978-1-4842-6158-3   ISBN-13 (electronic): 978-1-4842-6159-0
https://doi.org/10.1007/978-1-4842-6159-0

Managing Director, Apress Media LLC: Welmoed Spahr
Acquisitions Editor: Shiva Ramachandran
Development Editor: Rita Fernando
Coordinating Editor: Rita Fernando

Cover designed by eStudioCalamar

Distributed to the book trade worldwide by Springer Science+Business Media New York, 1 New York Plaza, New York, NY 100043. Phone 1-800-SPRINGER, fax (201) 348-4505, e-mail orders-ny@springer-sbm.com, or visit www.springeronline.com. Apress Media, LLC is a California LLC and the sole member (owner) is Springer Science + Business Media Finance Inc (SSBM Finance Inc). SSBM Finance Inc is a **Delaware** corporation.

For information on translations, please e-mail booktranslations@springernature.com; for reprint, paperback, or audio rights, please e-mail bookpermissions@springernature.com.

Apress titles may be purchased in bulk for academic, corporate, or promotional use. eBook versions and licenses are also available for most titles. For more information, reference our Print and eBook Bulk Sales web page at http://www.apress.com/bulk-sales.

Any source code or other supplementary material referenced by the author in this book is available to readers on GitHub via the book's product page, located at www.apress.com/9781484261583. For more detailed information, please visit http://www.apress.com/source-code.

Printed on acid-free paper

This book is dedicated to the hardworking board directors who take the time to continuously learn and understand disruptive forces, hold management accountable for their actions, and strive to set a culture in the organization that considers all stakeholder values.

Contents

About the Author. vii

Introduction ix

Chapter 1:   Old Rules vs. New Rules of Business 1

Chapter 2:   Why Nothing Changes – Status Quo at Work 19

Chapter 3:   Disruption and Digital Trends for the Next Decade. 29

Chapter 4:   Cybersecurity. 51

Chapter 5:   The Future of Work and Societal Shifts 83

Chapter 6:   Environmental and Social Governance 107

Chapter 7:   The Future of the Boardroom 121

Appendix A: Future Trends 159

References. 163

Index 191

About the Author

Jennifer C. Wolfe is an independent boardroom advisor to public and private companies and family-owned enterprises. As a corporate director, author, and thought leader, she helps boards maximize effectiveness in understanding future trends and disruptive forces. She has the distinction of serving as a faculty member and Board Leadership Fellow for the National Association of Corporate Directors.

Wolfe served as the managing partner of an intellectual property law firm she founded at the age of 28 in 2000 that grew into one of the top 75 patent law firms in the United States by 2015. The firm represented clients such as Microsoft, Adobe, Kroger, Procter & Gamble, Kraft Foods, Scripps Networks Interactive, Duke Energy, and other Fortune 500 companies. In 2012, Jen founded a digital agency to help c-suite executives prepare for digital and disruptive trends.

Disruption in the Boardroom is Jen's fifth book. Her prior works, *Brand Rewired*, *Domain Names Rewired*, *Digital in the Boardroom*, and *Blockchain in the Boardroom*, have been endorsed by senior executives from Microsoft, Procter & Gamble, Richemont, Warner Brothers, GE, the Motion Picture Association of America, Uber, and others. For more information about Jen, go to www.jenwolfe.com.

Introduction

One hundred years ago, the invention of the assembly line made new technologies affordable and ushered in an era of automobiles, refrigerators, and radios to connect to the world beyond. The economy was booming and the quality of life was improving, until it fell apart in 1929 when the stock market crashed and led to the Great Depression. At the time, the role of the board of directors in American corporations was largely ceremonial, and the quintessential good ol' boys club. Even after the regulatory changes to prevent another Depression, the board of directors essentially just "rubber-stamped" or automatically approved what management did. Since managers selected the directors, it was a fairly symbiotic relationship.

In the 1970s, however, the Securities and Exchange Commission brought corporate governance into a new age with reform to hold directors responsible for accurately representing the company's financial condition. It was at this time that the New York Stock Exchange required each corporation to have an audit committee composed of all independent board directors. The 1980s saw merger mania, and organizations like ISS (Institutional Shareholder Services) were formed to help shareholders with voting rights.

As the dot-com bubble began to go bust by the end of the 1990s, so did some other poor corporate governance practices. In 2001, revelations that Enron, WorldCom, Global Crossing, and Adelphia Communications had been defrauding investors together with self-dealing at Tyco, HealthSouth, and ImClone, Congress leapt into action. After the Enron scandal, Congress passed with overwhelming bipartisan support the Sarbanes–Oxley Act in 2002. A big part of this legislation was new corporate governance requirements for companies and boards including new independence rules for external auditors and a new regulator, the Public Company Accounting Oversight Board. At the same time, the two largest stock markets in the United States embarked on new self-regulatory requirements including an independent majority board, a Nomination and Governance committee comprised of independent directors; additional audit committee requirements; and executive session requirements for nonmanagement directors, that each company have an internal audit department and that each company disclose corporate governance guidelines including director qualifications and standards. Finally, CEO certification of the accuracy of information they provide was introduced to hold CEOs personally accountable.

When the financial crisis of 2008 hit, boards were once again under scrutiny. All of this was intended to overcome that "rubber-stamping" of management and create true independent oversight by boards to protect shareholders. Strong governance principles and an independent and diverse board would be demanded by both government and shareholders alike in the aftermath. Individual directors have more fiduciary responsibilities than directors of the past, and at least in theory, recruitment is based upon one's resume and experience. You'll notice almost all of this reform dealt with finance and transparency on accounting practices. These financial transparency–driven structural changes have shaped corporate governance practices for the last 100 years and particularly the last two decades.

But as we enter this next decade, technological changes create potentially dangerous unintended consequences, and as the pace of change accelerates, the role of the board of directors will again be reformed to meet new needs as stewards of good governance and oversight of management decisions. Sage counsel and the ability to see disruption and weigh potential unintended consequences will become part of the board's responsibility to protect not just shareholders but all stakeholders (employees, customers, vendors, strategic partners, the community in which it operates). By the end of the first quarter of 2020, it became clear that boards would be called upon for leadership to respond to an unprecedented global shutdown due to the coronavirus pandemic ("2020 Coronavirus Pandemic"). Forced into virtual-only meetings, boards struggled to address the needs of their stakeholders with a renewed understanding of their dependence on good supply chains. Boards rushed to weigh in on how to keep employees and customers healthy and safe and how to manage professionals now working from home. They had to immediately address cash flow, access to credit, how to manage their supply chain, whether or not to take stimulus money from the government if that was an option, whether or not to furlough employees, and what new modes of doing business would be required. Crisis management was no longer just an exercise to be held once a year, but the "new normal."

As the future is changing rapidly, we will need our leaders to have intellectual honesty to read and understand multiple points of view and trust but verify what they are being told by management. We need directors to have the moral courage to question assumptions and challenge old ideas, as well as stand up to charismatic leaders who mislead others for personal gain. We need directors and leaders who recognize we are in a perpetual state of change and who possess the discipline for constant learning about new technologies, security vulnerabilities, and societal shifts.

Twenty years ago, we witnessed the dawn of the digital age. Today, we are poised for a decade of setting the stage for what will come in the next modern age of enlightenment. Not unlike 1920, many of the technologies being developed today will require significant infrastructure and capital investment to bring to life the true potential benefits for humanity. And, we will need oversight to ensure corporations don't jeopardize our future with short-sighted decision making.

During the digital revolution of the last 20 years, audit and financial transparency along with CEO succession, executive compensation, and strategy to deliver short-term shareholder value has been the priority mission for corporate boards. But as we have watched systemic failures in companies like Wells Fargo, Equifax, Boeing, Theranos, and WeWork, it becomes clear another "Enron" moment is on the horizon. It is unclear if the 2020 Coronavirus Pandemic will slow or accelerate that moment or if it has simply been eclipsed by a global shutdown of society. Many of the disruptive changes already underway will be amplified, and boards need to be prepared to respond.

Cybersecurity threats are increasing while privacy demands become unrealistic, particularly in the new surveillance state in the name of public health and mass exodus of employees from the more secure office to working from home – all of this creates new points of vulnerability. Legislation and more regulation are pending to hold directors more responsible for security and privacy of consumers. Emerging technologies, rapidly changing business models, the changing workforce, and societal shifts threaten every organization in parallel with automation. Climate change and environmental issues, #metoo, and diversity amid a polarized political landscape leave even the most politically adept at a loss for words. Total disruption circles every industry. Something will break and change everything, and the 2020 Coronavirus Pandemic is a wake-up call. Governance of companies from startups to the Fortune 10 will be increasingly important in a complex and changing environment.

How can a group of 6–10 people be expected to oversee so much where the consequences can be devastating to more than just shareholders and mean more than just losing money? Will the role of the board evolve from arm's length oversight of largely accounting practices to accountability for management's actions and safeguarding all of its stakeholders?

An evolving framework for managing the future and culture of the organization from the boardroom is needed now more than ever. The role of the board and potentially even the regulatory structure of the board are due for disruption.

While the aim of this book is to share many cautionary tales of boards that have failed their stakeholders, I also recognize the incredible work being done by so many directors that never make the headlines or find their way into books like this. In the last chapter, I detail best practices and highlight how some boards are thinking disruptively and innovating to meet future demands.

If you are reading this book, you are likely the type of director who takes your role very seriously, does your homework, and asks challenging questions. But look around your boardroom table and your c-suite and ask yourself if everyone else does the same. If they don't, will you have the moral courage to address it before something goes wrong?

In the last 20 years of my career in leading an intellectual property law firm serving both startup tech companies and the biggest global consumer companies in the world, working globally in developing Internet policy, and building an advisory firm working with boards and c-suite executives to understand digital trends and cybersecurity threats, I've seen firsthand the challenges senior executives and boards face.

I've been in boardrooms around the world where some board members are conscientious about the changes occurring, but many others deny that it is happening or are not interested in hearing other viewpoints. I've been at a board meeting where a director nodded off to sleep. I've been at a board meeting where it was said they didn't need to worry about cybersecurity because they outsourced it. I've been at a board meeting where many of the things I detail as cautionary tales have happened.

In this book I have aggregated and anonymized anecdotal evidence of the pending disruption. If it is based upon public information or I quote a statistic or person, I have cited sources by chapter in the "References" section. Based upon extensive research and interviews, this book will detail what we can learn from past mistakes, what trends we can expect to see develop over the next decade, and how to structure future governance to meet changing demands.

You may not agree with my opinion on everything in this book, and that's a good thing. There are many opinions on future trends, how technologies will work, and what unintended consequences may arise. There are also differing views on the role of the board. I've pulled research from top institutions on best practices and forward thinking about good governance. I hope this book will provide you insights into good questions to ask and things to think about as you prepare for strategic planning and serve as a discussion starting point in your boardroom.

In this book, I'll cover several key concepts:

- Chapter 1, Old Rules vs. New Rules of Business: How the underlying business models have shifted and what we need to do in the decades ahead to blend the best of both worlds.

- Chapter 2, Why Nothing Changes – Status Quo at Work: Too many organizations have the wrong incentives, designed for the pace of business two decades ago.

- Chapter 3, Disruption and Digital Trends for the Next Decade: What you need to know in the boardroom about what's coming in layman's terms.

- Chapter 4, Cybersecurity: Everything we do creates new vulnerabilities; how do you manage this when you don't even know what threatens you?

- Chapter 5, The Future of Work and Societal Shifts: Millennials and Gen Z are our future leaders amid a profound shift in how we all live and work. How will you cultivate a path for them to lead the organization of the future?

- Chapter 6, Environmental and Social Governance: Climate change, #metoo, and diversity, amid political polarization are all new issues in the boardroom. We are in one of the most divided times in history; how do we balance out so many competing needs and be good stewards to benefit all stakeholders?

- Chapter 7, The Future of the Boardroom: A practical framework for managing a vast new world of technology, cybersecurity, and societal shifts and the important leadership role the board of directors has as our protectors. The old structure of the board may not work in the decade ahead. I know that no one likes to change. But disruption is the new normal, which means the boardroom must change with it.

After initially writing this book, a global disruption of unfathomable scale occurred, the 2020 Coronavirus Pandemic. In the editing process, I have added references to the pandemic and how it has impacted boardroom discussions and practices. In many ways, what has happened has reinforced many of the disruptive trends, and best practices are already underway. As in many areas of business, trends that were developing have been amplified and accelerated – the same is true in the boardroom.

The boardroom is overdue for disruption and changes to the very way it operates in our new era of the fourth industrial revolution. The 2020 Coronavirus Pandemic forced some change, but long-lasting change is coming in the next decade. Will your board be ready?

Old Rules vs. New Rules of Business

How the underlying business models have shifted and what we need to do in the decades ahead to blend the best of both worlds.

We need good corporate governance now more than ever which requires directors to embrace

1. Intellectual honesty
2. Moral courage
3. Discipline for continuous learning

We'll go through each attribute in this chapter and in Chapters 2 and 3. Let's start with intellectual honesty. To embrace your **intellectual honesty**, you *must seek out more than one opinion on issues, challenge your own assumptions, accept that your long-held beliefs may no longer be accurate in a changing world, be honest with yourself when faced with new information, embrace change and be confident enough to accept when you are on the wrong path in order to course correct, and don't hide the truth from yourself or allow hypocrisy to fool you.*

© Jennifer C. Wolfe 2020
J. C. Wolfe, *Disruption in the Boardroom*, https://doi.org/10.1007/978-1-4842-6159-0_1

To be prepared for the disruption coming in business and in the boardroom, we need to start by reflecting on the underpinnings of the business models that have shaped our modern times, what drives innovation and disruption, as well as the mistakes that have permeated our corporate culture in the last 20 years. Historical perspective can help us see what's coming and how to be prepared, as well as make smart decisions about how to structure the boardroom for the future. All of my references and citations are included in the "References" section of the book.

"Old Rules"

Since the industrial revolution, corporations were built on a few fundamental principles, long taught at prestigious Ivy League business schools. Scholars like Michael Porter, Peter Drucker, and Jim Collins have lectured these tenets and become the framework for leaders on today's corporate boards. Certain truths and assumptions were the bedrock of business strategy and principles. Stalwart companies were built brick by brick and policy by policy on what was tried and true even as times and technology changed:

- Make a product or deliver a service that meets a need in the marketplace at the right price for market conditions.

- Manage your operations efficiently and keep costs under control.

- Create a long-term path for your employees based upon trust and loyalty.

- Earn a profit and produce shareholder value.

- Manage risk and create sustainability and growth for shareholders.

For Baby Boomers (born between 1944 and 1964) and Gen Xers (those born from 1965 to 1979), these were the principles taught to them in business school and reinforced early in their career. According to the National Association of Corporate Directors (NACD), the average age of a corporate director is 63.1. This means the people providing oversight to American corporations were educated and found success operating under these "old rules." But this model lacks incentive for innovation for the sake of innovation – something we wouldn't fully recognize we needed until the early 2000s.

In the first half of the twentieth century, AT&T built a hive of innovation known as Bell Labs. In fact, Bell Labs invested in technologies that would later become the foundation to our digital age. For example, early lasers, cell phone networks, digital processors, fiber optic networks, and satellites were all initially developed and patented within the safe innovation space of Bell Labs. Sheltered from competition as a monopoly, the company could truly innovate without the need to roll out its inventions as profitable products, much like modern-day Silicon Valley (backed by venture capital money). They didn't have to market and sell their new inventions profitably because they had the safety of running a monopoly phone system. The ability to innovate free from that pressure that was baked into their business model. This continued until 1984, when the US government splintered AT&T as a monopoly, bringing about the beginning of the end of Bell Labs. Some believe that we subsequently lost an important research lab, while others believe it spawned the birth of the startup culture as new entrepreneurial ventures replaced the old "labs" concept.

Companies with foundations back to the early 1900s like Procter & Gamble, Kodak, Kellogg, Folgers, Kimberly-Clark, General Mills, Ford, Coca-Cola, Pepsi, Johnson & Johnson, Kraft, and others would also innovate, but most for many decades still had to fit those innovative products within the old constructs of business (i.e., it needed to be profitable to roll out). This meant change moved at a slower pace for most of the last century because ideas were fully vetted and tested before rolled out and consumer adoption was slow. There was no social media to virally spread new products or ideas, so everything took longer.

Even as new companies like Microsoft, Oracle, Sun, Intel, and ultimately Apple emerged in the early stages of the technology age in the 1970s and 1980s, innovation had to be funneled into profitable ventures or they would not survive. Even Apple nearly went bankrupt before reemerging as the powerhouse it is today. When Steve Jobs returned to the company after a decade of separation in 1997, he moved quickly with iMac, iTunes, and iPod and started the resurgence to what it is today. But he had to be profitable to compete.

On Fox Business News on November 14 of 2019, former Microsoft CEO, Steve Ballmer said: "At Microsoft, we never lost money, not one year, it's different than today's Silicon Valley."

In the late 1980s and early 1990s, the Internet began to emerge from academic and government backrooms where only the highly technical could access it into mainstream consumer households as a centerpiece of daily life. By the late 1990s, new business models were beginning to form, creating "new rules" of business in stark contrast to what had been taught and disciplined into American corporate culture. Rules that had dominated generations of business were suddenly claimed to be obsolete and lack vision for the future. Companies like Amazon and Google were started and operated with new ideas and rules about how companies would grow.

An all too eager venture capital industry was building momentum on the idea that nine out of ten of their entrepreneurial companies would fail, but if that one could IPO with a big enough valuation, it would offset the other losses and be the win they needed to keep going. At the same time, the Internet democratized investment in the stock market. As platforms like E-Trade gave individuals the ability to invest their retirement savings directly vs. through a broker, something important began to happen. Investment in companies was no longer just for big-wig financiers. The average person could participate in buying stock and growing their portfolio. And, the idea that a guy in a garage could become Steve Jobs, a billionaire, captured the imagination of inventors alongside investors looking for the next big thing. Investors would prop up these companies and their "new rules" and help them survive where any other company would have failed.

The rules of business for these "new economy" companies, as it was referred to in the early 2000s, changed the fundamentals of what was considered good business practices.

And then the establishment, the companies that had been around for generations were caught off guard. They couldn't compete under these "new rules." They had no venture capitalist propping them up. They had to be profitable or their share price would tumble, and banks would pull their lines of credit. At the same time, with these new investors buying and selling stock directly and, ultimately, algorithms driving stock market prices in often irrational ways responding to data inputs, the large companies became more focused on short-term profitability. This is important because it means "New Rule" companies were emerging without being profitable, but were dramatically changing the way people lived with their innovative thinking and the "Old Rule" companies were under more pressure than ever to be profitable, crippling their ability to innovate for the sake of innovation, until they had to.

"New Rules"

The "New Rules" of business were in stark contrast to what had long been considered best practices:

- Give away your product for "free."

- Move-fast-and-break-things culture.

- Invest hundreds of millions in venture capital and don't worry about making money — build the product and profitability will come.

- Claim a multibillion-dollar value before you are profitable.

- Don't Own Anything. Uber, for example, doesn't own the cars or even employ the drivers. Airbnb doesn't own the homes it rents. WeWork doesn't own the office space it rents.

- Circumvent local rules, regulations, and taxes so you can beat out traditional competitors before they can catch up to your new ideas.

- Spy on your customers and then sell their data to try to make money.

- Cash out with an IPO, become a billionaire yourself, and figure the rest out later.

These New Rules allow for scaled innovation of new ideas that transform our world but aren't sustainable indefinitely. And, the unintended consequences almost always hurt more than just the investors.

Despite the dot-com bubble bursting in 2000, many of these "new rule" companies survived. Those that did would change everything. Google, Amazon, Netflix, Facebook, and Twitter thrived and have become so powerful that today they all face potential government intervention in their business due to a convergence of privacy concerns and antitrust charges for buying up companies that could create competition.

But many like Webvan, eToys.com, Pets.com, Broadcast.com, and thousands more all crashed and burned, leaving investors with nothing. While many argue we need this model to create the next Google, Amazon, or Facebook, others question the viability and the negative implications of the irrational exuberance of the dot-com era. But, let's continue on with a bit of history before we make any judgment calls on what models are likely to survive in the decade ahead, now dubbed the fourth industrial revolution.

We have this perfect storm happening in the years since the dot-com bubble burst.

- Well-funded startups propped up by big venture capital money are rewriting the rules and don't have to be profitable to be considered successful – unicorn CEOs attain cult-like followings.

- The established companies that need to be profitable and operate under old rules are desperate to respond with their own innovation and yet under more pressure than ever from Wall Street for short-term gains creating a disincentive for the establishment to invest in innovation for the sake of innovation at the time they needed it the most.

During this time, boards were still performing largely "traditional" roles of audit, CEO succession, and approving mergers, acquisitions, and the company's overarching strategy. To be fair, it is not the board's role to run the company, their job is oversight. But as the rules of business were changing around them and their structure and role insulated them, problems emerged. What follows are a just a few of many stories that provide lessons for boards.

Case Studies: What Could Go Wrong Under the Shifting Rules of Business?

Old Rule–Driven Companies Miss Key Opportunities, Lack Vision, or Break Rules out of Desperation

Companies that were well established before the dot-com boom were often blinded by their own false assumptions as disruption circled. Let's look at a few of the bigger blunders from "Old Rule" companies of the last two decades and find key takeaways to consider in today's climate. Consider these case studies in the context of what you may be facing in your boardroom today. Are there any lessons you can learn to build out reasonable assumptions about the future? Research supporting these case studies is included in the "References" section for further reading.

Blockbuster, as the predominant player in the distribution of home video through the 1980s and 1990s, had the opportunity to buy Netflix in 2000 for $50 million. Today, Netflix is worth a purported $125 billion. Where was the board of directors when that decision was being made? Why did they miss the signals that everything was about to change? Are you missing those signals today? Most reporting of the Blockbuster story has been done with the benefit of hindsight vs. recognizing it at the time (showing a more systemic lack of vision in media and business), but it is clear their leaders and their board didn't really understand the coming digital age, let alone the eventual streaming wars that would follow. Perhaps this is why big tech have so quickly gobbled up any company that could compete it with (i.e., Facebook acquiring Instagram and WhatsApp). Ironically, that is also now what leads them to potential antitrust investigations. After all, Blockbuster probably would have killed Netflix instead of allowing it to grow and thrive. Blockbuster was eventually sold to dish out of bankruptcy court for $320 million in 2011, with the brand largely dead.

Kodak, the inventor of modern photography, had been a household name for decades creating "Kodak Moments." However, the name is less known among younger generations because the board didn't respond to the digital photography revolution. Management had the opportunity but simply declined to accept digital photography as a disruptive force even as its own researchers and intelligence experts presented the reality to senior leaders. In fact, Kodak invented digital photography – they owned the original patents on it. This is an important point. Inside the company, researchers and those responsible for helping to predict future trends *were not* listened to by senior executives and the board. These insiders cautioned leaders that they had ten years before the transformation would occur. They were right, but management and the board only wanted to reinforce their views of the company's dominance in the industry, they didn't want to see or believe a future that was not consistent with their existing assumptions. They weren't looking at what could put them out of business, they simply didn't think it could happen. It's really that simple. It wasn't some grand strategy that went wrong, it's that they just didn't want to accept change. Senior leaders and board directors need to embrace change, push their assumptions, and accept that we live in a time of profound transformation which will continue at an accelerating pace. Those who don't adapt will die.

Wells Fargo is a company proud of its local banking heritage going back over a century, even marketing itself with the logo of a horse-drawn wagon defining it as a legacy bank that you could trust. Yet, as pressure mounted for profitability and sales goals, things went vastly wrong. Deep in the organization, the sales goals for employees were so out of whack with what was realistic that they resorted to fraudulent practices. In the investigations since, it has become clear there was a systemic cultural failure. Congress has called senior executives before committee after committee to explain what happened and how they could have failed their customers and the public so egregiously. Where was leadership? Where was the board of directors when all of this happened? I've talked about this case study at boardroom leadership programs and asked these exact questions to the attendees. Some board members raised their hand to offer the opinion "that the board could not possibly know what the compensation structure was for employees so deep in the organization." "They [the board] are only responsible for compensation of key executives," it has been said. However, in the aftermath, the board does need to understand the culture of the organization. And, in fact, it was uncovered that the board was aware of the problem. Regulators agree and are holding senior executives personally and financially accountable with steep personal penalties. US regulators sought $59 million in fines from the bank's former CEO, general counsel, chief auditor, audit director, and community banking risk officer. According to Bloomberg, they "created a culture of fear." The Office of the Comptroller of Currency released a statement, "Hundreds of thousands of employees in the banks largest line of business engaged in systemic illegal activity for 14 years." In its complaint, it states that the board concluded "the only way to definitively address the broken sales model and the root cause of the sales practices was to emphasize other metrics for performance and to abandon exerting pressure through sales goals and sales driven incentive programs." The complaint finds that these practices continued for 14 years. "It took a massive failure on the part of the senior management, the law department and audit for the sales practices misconduct problem to become as severe and pervasive at it was and last as long as it did." Even after that, the regulators found that senior executives provided misleading and incomplete reporting to the board and that the problem was not actually solved until there was intense congressional interest and public outcry. If the board doesn't hold management responsible for setting that tone and culture or checking and knowing what's going on at the front lines, then who will? It's no longer acceptable for boards to say, "they didn't know," or that "they were being misled by management." The evolving role of the board will be to trust but verify and know what's going on in the company it oversees.

Equifax is the keeper of our financial credit score, our most prized information that we need to buy a home, a car, start a business, just about anything requiring a loan. And yet, in 2017 they breached that trust when they failed to patch a known open source code vulnerability – a patch that was free, by the way. As the Equifax security breach was detailed in forensic studies, it became clear they didn't have the right leadership or process in place. They are not alone. I've done a lot of work with companies in implementing open source compliance programs. The reality is that every company is using open source code in some form or another either directly or through vendors. Most digital apps and software are built using at least some open source code. This means there must be some tracking of it and tracking of the patches that are needed when vulnerabilities are discovered (this is true in other software, too, but it is particularly important with open source code). In the open source community, patches are shared freely. It just takes someone inside your organization tracking it and then patching it. It's not expensive or difficult if you have the right processes in place. When it comes to Equifax, it turns out their head of security was a music major in college. Not to say you can't learn and develop the skills you need later in life, but it appears, she didn't quite have the expertise she needed. In scathing articles about the breach, reporters questioned how the CEO could put someone without the right qualifications in charge of the company's data security. The failings put 143 million people at risk from identity theft and fraud. And too many other leaders simply assumed she had this covered. The CEO ultimately resigned under public pressure. The board surely didn't know or understand the risk of not patching open source code. Some have said this is not the purview of the board. But, after Equifax, it has to be. There's no excuse to not ask the questions of your management team: "Do we use open source code, do our vendors, how do we track it, how do we patch it, how do we know when new vulnerabilities exist?" If you are wondering what other types of questions you should be asking, then you're headed in the right direction. Check Chapter 4 for more details on cybersecurity questions to ask. The point here is, it's no longer okay for directors to not understand these issues, to not question what's happening, and to not have the intellectual honesty to recognize when they don't know what they don't know. And, make sure the people you hire are qualified to manage the technical issues impacting every organization.

Boeing. As I write this chapter, the scrutiny of Boeing leadership by government officials and the public is growing. The tragic crashes in 2019 of two Boeing 737 Max jets that killed everyone aboard thrust the company into the spotlight. Investigations revealed a number of problems. The software and artificial intelligence (AI) combined with a faulty sensor and the inability of pilots to correct the course of the plane resulted in the crashes. Further investigation showed that the company didn't believe simulator training was needed for pilots and offered certain simulator training as "extras" to sell to airlines. While it raised many questions about automation going too far (see more in Chapter 3 about this), the role of the board was to ensure a company that produces jets and sells them to the world's airlines rolls out new technology with proper safety features as a cornerstone, not an afterthought to profitability. While it's true, "old rule" companies are built on the bedrock of profitability, public safety, and worker safety must be part of the equation. There were immediate calls for the CEO to resign and some journalists calling for resignation of board members. This type of public outcry when companies choose profits over safety will continue. Tesla and Uber have also had fatal crashes from their "driverless cars" often when the safety driver just wasn't paying attention and a sensor or software didn't work as expected. But there was not a similar demand from the public for the resignations of their CEO or board members – perhaps because we are desensitized to car crashes as more frequent and airplane crashes strike a fear and nerve in us with heightened reactions. The reality is somewhere the culture in Boeing was responding to demands for sales at a faster pace than could be done safely and demands for increased revenue plagued the organizational thinking.

Of course, there are many examples of "old rule" companies that go out of business for a variety of reasons: Sears, Lehman Brothers, Toys "R" Us, Enron, Schwinn, Reader's Digest, TV Guide, Palm, Compaq, and so many others. While the reasons may be the company had run its life cycle, a forensic study typically leads back to turning points when the wrong decision was made by senior executives and the board about risk. Whether the management team misled the board, or the board didn't know what questions to ask, somewhere a systemic failure in these companies occurred in failing to see the future, failing to identify vulnerabilities, or pushing boundaries of profitability beyond what was reasonable. The directors of these companies move on and are often sought-after directors because of their experience, hopefully not repeating the same mistakes.

There are many legacy companies still operating under "Old Rules" trying to change course like GE, Macy's, Lego, Best Buy, Nintendo, GM, and so many others. In many instances, these companies continue to replace senior executives with insiders who have long held the same beliefs as their predecessors and continue to replace board directors with carbon copies of those who leave.

It's fair to question if the discussion in the boardroom will change if the people sitting at the table have all had the same experiences. It's not exclusively about race or gender anymore (though that remains important), but about diversity of experience and thought. Most boards recruit prior CEOs or CFOs of large conglomerates, or similarly sized companies and industries. *If the whole board is filled with the same basic resume and skill set, how do you expect the discussion to change?*

General Magic was a company caught in between the shift from "Old Rules" to "New Rules." Their story is simple and yet prophetic. In the early 1990s, they had the idea of a modern-day smart phone, but the technology wasn't quite fully developed yet. They were a spin off from Apple, and as they needed funding, they partnered up with established players like AT&T and Sony. But AT&T and Sony were not funding a "Bell Labs," they needed a product that could be sold and drive their profit-focused business models. When General Magic still needed more money for development of the product than AT&T or Sony could provide, they became the first company to IPO pre-revenue or profitability and raised more money. And then, Apple launched the Newton as a competitive product, putting pressure on the General Magic engineers from AT&T and Sony to get to market before they were ready. There was one other thing the founders and the hardworking engineers missed. The Internet was starting to form, and the way people lived was about to change. But, their idea of a smart phone was ten years too early for society. The technology was not quite able to deliver something user friendly enough at a price point that would work at the time. Ultimately ending in bankruptcy, many of the early employees and engineers would go on to found eBay, work at Google in leadership roles, be part of the invention team at Apple on the iPod and iPhone, as well as found and invent the Nest thermostat (i.e., the beginning of smart everything) and sell it to Google for billions. Their story is important because as they were caught between the shifting business models at the turn of the century, they made the same mistakes many continue to make today. It also reinforces the importance of companies allowing some spaces for innovation to occur, much like Bell Labs, that doesn't require an immediate return on investment. Imagine, for example, if Sony or AT&T had allowed them to continue their work without the profit pressure, they might have beat Apple to the smart phone.

The common thread among these established companies is that senior leaders and the board of directors didn't seek out multiple sources of information, didn't challenge what they were being told, or in some cases, listen to what they were being told when it was different than what they believed. These are good case studies for board directors to reflect upon and consider if their company is an "Old Rule" business model and question how they navigate to avoid these disruptive failures. Let's take a look at a few "New Rule" companies and how they are facing their own challenges in the boardroom.

"New Rule" Companies Simply Break the Rules

Companies that have emerged since 2000 have been built upon "New Rule" business models. But, in many ways, they are breaking all the rules which result in unintended consequences. Even in startup companies that grow rapidly, the role of the board of directors is to oversee the scaled innovation and disruption to ensure that stakeholders are protected. *Stakeholders* means not just investors or shareholders but also customers, employees, vendors, and strategic partners. When the other senior leaders and directors do not have the moral courage to challenge irresponsible behavior by a smooth-talking CEOs, we have a recipe for disaster. Let's look at a few of the bigger ones.

Theranos, the entrepreneurial company that was going to change the health-care industry, is the story of a charismatic CEO who was smart enough to enlist a prestigious board of directors including the likes of Henry Kissinger, James Mattis, and George Schulz, now widely known because of the book *Bad Blood* by John Carreyrou and HBO's documentary *The Inventor: Out for Blood*. In the aftermath of the expose, it is easy to see that Elizabeth Holmes was blinding her board and leveraging tough tactic lawyering to prevent the truth from coming to light. She had an idea, which while innovative was flawed on many levels. The idea was to take a small sample of blood at a local drug store, like Walgreens, where testing could be done on a variety of health factors in the pharmacy with just a few drops of blood instead of multiple samples taken at the doctor. The immediate results could be provided direct to the consumer.

Holmes masterfully raised money and built a lab and a team of people who would hide her secret. She charmed a board of directors into her vision for the future and found herself on the cover of magazines like *Forbes*, *Fortune*, and *Inc.* as one of the first self-made billionaire women. Sporting black turtlenecks to channel Steve Jobs like belief in her abilities, she hid the truth. The technology didn't work. It wasn't possible to test so many different potential illnesses or problems in a small test tube taken in a drug store. It wasn't a matter of not seeing the future, but that the technology didn't really work. Until the very end, she convinced companies like Walgreens; Walmart; Oracle founder, Larry Ellison; Rupert Murdoch; and education secretary, Betsy DeVos; among other billionaires to believe her story. Ultimately, whistleblowers like Tyler Schultz had the moral courage to fight the bullying of Theranos' powerhouse legal team and tell the truth. Holmes faces criminal charges of fraud, wire fraud, and conspiracy to commit wire fraud in a trial that could result in up to 20 years in prison. Why did the board not know? Why did they allow bullying lawyers to prevent at least an internal investigation? Why was this one woman granted so much power? Why did the media fall for it? In these companies driven by charismatic leaders with the promise of greatness and billions of dollars in returns for investors, directors need to be sure a few fundamental questions are answered – such as does the product actually work? Could it cause harm or death to innocent people if it doesn't?

WeWork's, Adam Neumann was building his empire of a technology real estate company that would change how people work and live their life. With lofty aspirations as a self-proclaimed "unicorn," SoftBank backed the company despite the reality that the numbers just never worked. That backing and a desire to not miss out on the next IPO, JP Morgan CEO Jamie Dimon dove into the deep end of the pool with WeWork. In the aftermath, Dimon said on CNBC in November of 2019, "I think there are lessons to be learned about these valuations, how you go public, and how you treat the public shareholder." Following the "New Rules" of business, the idea to grow and innovate for the sake of growth blinded the board and other carefully chosen followers in the organization. Neumann trademarked the word "WE" in his own personal name and then attempted to sell it to the company for $6 million dollars. In the same vein, Neumann was borrowing hundreds of millions of dollars using his shares of WeWork as collateral to buy buildings and then lease them back to WeWork all while the company, itself, was not profitable. Has anyone on their board ever heard of a conflict of interest? You don't have to be a lawyer to see the problem here. And further investigation into the board turns up all types of potential conflicts of interest among the other board members, which could explain why they looked the other way.

Even if the board didn't think there was a conflict of interest, maybe they should check their math. The basic premise of the business was to lease up expensive real estate, make it "cool" as a place to work, and then sublease it out with short-term leases to companies, often startup companies. While certainly the design styles might be hip and cool, there were problems in the execution of the plan. Many reports cite that the information technology network infrastructure was cheaply done, weak, and vulnerable by even the most liberal of standards. Many said it was a "joke" and easy to hack. WeWork was also trying to save money by purchasing inexpensive phone booths made in China. It turns out the material not only gave off a foul odor but was a carcinogen. Pregnant women who made calls in the phone booths were outraged they were not informed. While going cheap on the phone booths for their tenants, Neumann was out purchasing a private jet for hundreds of millions so he and his family could fly around to his many homes on his surfing expeditions. So, the network installed for tenants leaves them vulnerable to a cyberattack and the materials used to create phone booths could cause cancer, but the CEO is flying around in a private jet to go surfing. Sounds like a good use of company funds.

How did no one have the moral courage to stand up to this and say something? While it is true it is a privately held company, the intention to become public meant there needed to be some oversight, and a board of directors ensuring this kind of malfeasance was not tolerated. And as they approached IPO positioning, many began to question the faulty accounting and creative means of trying to show a path to profitability. The basic math of the equation showed they couldn't climb out of their hole. They don't own the real estate, they just lease it, and when there isn't enough money to pay the leases, they will be out of business. Now factor in a global pandemic that shuts down businesses; those short-term leases may not be renewed. There was actually no technology to their "technology" company other than cheap IT infrastructure that they bought from someone else and installed poorly. Hanging by a thread with SoftBank doubling down, we will see what happens to WeWork. Many believe it can be turned around. But it isn't even an innovative idea. Subleasing real estate has been around for a long time, it just hasn't been masqueraded as a tech company worth billions. It's a reasonably good business if done properly. Certainly, the idea of community-driven workplaces makes sense and will likely grow after the pandemic. How did the board of directors allow the CEO to cash out while investors and employees were left with nothing? How is that effective oversight? As the 2020 Coronavirus Pandemic further damaged the office space company, how should the board react? Should they claw back the money? Will they be sued if they do not? These are all questions directors should be contemplating in normal times, but at a heightened level during unprecedented calamities like the global shutdown caused by Coronavirus.

Over at **Uber**, the company is still not profitable after a disappointing IPO and the former CEO has resigned from the board and sold all of his shares of stock. The company's mission was clearly visionary in creating a new model of transportation – on-demand transportation using shared resources. They quickly captured market share by scaling globally via venture capital money. With dominance in almost every market, they are still not yet profitable. How will that work when they are about to face a whole series of costly problems, even before the global shutdown occurred? The company grew quickly by circumventing what traditional taxi and car service companies had built into their cost structure. They didn't hire employees, so they didn't pay payroll taxes. They didn't have to buy tax medallions or follow local regulations regarding licensure to drive strangers around. The result? In 2019, 6000 women were raped in Uber cars just in the United States. The numbers in places like India are far worse. Is there possibly a reason drivers need to be licensed and registered to drive the public? Any chance there was a public interest in having that type of regulation? If they already have market dominance and aren't profitable and their cost structure is about to increase, how does the math work there without some very creative accounting (i.e., remember Enron)?

The same can be said of **Airbnb**. Is there a health code to be followed when you just randomly rent out your home? What about a prohibition against cameras? Many Airbnb homes have been found to have cameras watching guests while the owners are away. What about local tourism taxes that support the local community? It has certainly created an industry around short-term rentals, but there are consequences of rapid growth without following the rules that have been set up for the industries these innovative companies disrupt. While it allows for scaled innovation, it also creates new problems to address. In the aftermath of the 2020 Coronavirus Pandemic, Airbnb may find more local municipalities or communities banning short-term rentals.

Uber has also banked heavily in its investment in driverless cars, but there are years of challenges to driverless cars to address before that even becomes a possibility (see Chapter 3). If you were on their board, what questions would you be asking? What about their corporate culture? In response to a whistleblower outing a frat boy culture and raising concerns about a sexually hostile work environment toward women, the board opted to hire former Attorney General Eric Holder to assess and advise on creating a better culture. It was criticized after the report came out that the investigation focused too much on boilerplate workplace culture with issues of sexual harassment, and discrimination taking a back seat, Dan Primack of Axios said, "In trying to fix the company's culture in this manner, its board put employee moral through extra degradation and risked shareholder value. If this was crisis management 101, Uber flunked the test." Was that sufficient? Hiring a well-known politician may make for good headlines, but is it really solving the problem? Travis Kalanick has cashed out. Would that concern you if you were on this board?

Another example to showcase how things go wrong in "New Rule" companies is **Outcome Health** in Chicago. The concept was simple, they would place flat screen televisions into patient rooms at doctor's offices and run ads by pharmaceuticals. Sounds like a reasonable business, but is that ethical? Do we really want ads forced on us in the most vulnerable moment when we are being examined by a doctor? Save that ethical question for later because it's so much more than just that. Founders Shradha Agarwal and Rishi Shah quickly secured big investors from Goldman Sachs, Google, and other investment bankers to the tune of hundreds of millions of dollars. They quickly expanded with hundreds of employees and a valuation in the billions. Mayor Rahm Emanuel of Chicago appeared at a press conference at the opening of their new office building with expectations of hiring 2000 new employees. Except, it turns out, that it was all a scam. They were charging pharmaceuticals for ads being run on flat screens that were never installed. It was all fraudulent, sound familiar? As of this writing, the two founders were indicted for fraud, bank fraud, and money laundering. They face up to 30 years in prison. How do established companies like Goldman Sachs, Google, and others end up involved in these types of ventures?

Even some of the original "tech" companies have had their share of failures and blind belief in the company talking points. Take **Yahoo!**, for example. Yahoo passed up the chance to buy Google for $1 billion in 2002. Despite its status as a "New Economy" company, its executives dragged their feet uncertain of Google's future and the price of Google soared out of reach. In July 2016, 22 years after it began, Yahoo agreed to sell its core operating business to Verizon in what Forbes writer Brian Solomon called "the saddest $5 billion deal in tech history."

Before Google or Facebook, Yahoo was the king of the Internet. Jeremy Ring, a top sales executive at Yahoo from 1996 to 2001 recalls the history in his memoir, *We Were Yahoo!*. He details the improbable rise and precipitous fall of what was once the biggest Internet company on the planet, worth $125 billion at its height. "Our company was five years old," Ring wrote. "We were worth more than Ford, Chrysler, and GM combined. Hell, we were worth more than Disney, Viacom, and News Corp combined. Each of those great American brands could have been swallowed up by us."

Except it wasn't and that's really the whole point. This was simply what their executives and backers believed and tried to convince everyone else was true — no different than what we continue to see today in "New Rule" companies. Whether it's Elizabeth Holmes or Adam Neumann, a charismatic CEO seems to blind board members. Believing their "New Rule" oversized, unrealistic valuations, executives made mistake and after mistake. Propped up for years by the large stake in Alibaba, eventually Yahoo would be swallowed up by Verizon at a fraction of its heyday value. Verizon ultimately took a multibillion-dollar write-down calling defeat on its Yahoo and AOL acquisitions.

A long list of popular companies remain teetering on the edge of profitability or plagued with problems, Snapchat and Twitter, to name two of the more popular. Will they survive the next decade? Will the 2020 Coronavirus Pandemic accelerate the bankruptcy of stale business models? Will their boards step in and course correct with new leadership, strategy, or approaches, or is it simply impossible to do so? Or, will they all, as they predict, become then next Google, Facebook, or Amazon?

Conclusion

In both *old rule* and *new rule* companies, we can see the flaws in the models. Old Rules focus on profitability at the expense of innovation. New Rules blind leaders to fundamental business principles with outsized valuations and unintended consequences. While it is true the CEO and the management team are responsible for executing on the strategy, the board is there to provide oversight and independent thinking and look out for red flags. If the board doesn't, who will?

Naturally, a CEO might not want to believe that the company he or she runs will be out of business, but the board should be able to look for signals and help the CEO see multiple points of view. You can't simply believe nothing will change and ignore the signals. And at the same time, you can be so overly exuberant about changing the world with your company that you ignore the fundamentals. There is an important blend of these models that will emerge in the decade ahead. Many might argue that companies like Google, Facebook, and Amazon have blended those models, and that's what accounts for their success. And some "old rule" companies have allowed for innovation to occur so they can thrive.

The role of the board here is critical – it's oversight. In each of these case studies in "old rule" or "new rule" companies, ask yourself:

- Should the board have known?
- Were they properly overseeing the culture that led to these incidents?
- Were they getting independent and objective perspective on what senior management told them?
- Should the board have taken action?
- Did senior executives mislead the board?
- Would that make a difference?
- Does the role of the board need to change in the aftermath of these lessons learned?

We need our senior leaders and board directors to have intellectual honesty and moral courage to address the shift that is underway. As business finds its way into a blend of old rules (i.e., operate profitability and with a fiduciary duty to stakeholders) with new rules (innovate and grow at a scaled pace), the business model of this century balancing fundamentals of disciplined business practices with strategic innovation labs will begin to emerge with the board of directors in a more critical role than ever. And, that role is in a state of evolution (or some might say disruption).

This chapter is a cautionary tale of the things that have gone wrong in the last 20 years as case studies directors can use to learn from and as guidance.

The boardroom will be disrupted this decade. It began with the 2020 Coronavirus Pandemic and will continue with the technological shifts that are already underway. Many of the trends addressed in this book will be amplified and accelerate because of the pandemic. Others may be slowed as a result of a global shutdown. If boards don't disrupt the way they do things themselves, the public may demand it if they think the company cares only about shareholders and not all the stakeholders. Lawmakers may regulate greater accountability from directors when they believe the public good is at stake. The "Old Rules" of business can blind leaders to change and the "New Rules" can also betray us with unintended consequences. To provide leadership and oversight in such a volatile time with new skills and knowledge needed, directors will need new tools, access to objective information, new structures, and governance framework.

Discussion Questions for the Boardroom

1. How has your company evolved from "old rules" to "new rules" of business?

    a. How will you blend profitability goals and responsibility with the demand for scaled innovation? Does it have to be one or the other?

2. How do you create safe spaces for innovation to occur?

3. How do you hold each other accountable for intellectual honesty?

4. Do you hold management accountable and verify the veracity of what they tell you?

5. How do you get other opinions that might challenge what you are thinking?

6. Do you always argue both sides of an issue before making a decision, particularly mergers and acquisitions?

    a. If everyone on your board agrees, do you seek out the alternative before moving forward to avoid making a mistake?

7. How do you ensure a problem is really solved after it is brought to your attention (i.e., Wells Fargo)?

8. Do you insist that new and objective outside counsel or consultants assess the effectiveness of how a cultural problem has been solved?

9. Do you get independent assessments of your cybersecurity protocols?

10. Do you have lists of new advisors or counsel you can call on who you have not worked with in the past when you need a fresh look at an issue?

11. Do you have a crisis communication plan if your company is accused of wrongdoing?

    a. Sexual harassment by senior officials

    b. Cybersecurity breach

    c. Bad sales practices or customer practices

12. Do you use artificial intelligence to analyze employee emails for potential problems?

    a. For example, Boeing might have discovered problems.

13. What sources of information do you use to determine if cultural problems exist?

14. Do you regularly use your product? Do you shop your own customer experience regularly to know what customers are experiencing? For example, did anyone on the Theranos board actually compare the results of a blood test from the product with one from a doctor? Did anyone on Uber's board actually talk to the women who had been raped or attacked inside the company? Did anyone on Blockbuster's board try Netflix to see what it was about?

15. Do you regularly discuss how your product could have adverse impacts on people and what you would do about it?

Why Nothing Changes – Status Quo at Work

Too many organizations have the wrong incentives, designed for the pace of business two decades ago.

As discussed in Chapter 1, we need good corporate governance now more than ever, and we must have intellectual honesty, moral courage, and discipline for continuous learning. In this chapter, we'll talk about moral courage as a fundamental principle of good governance.

1. **Moral courage** is *the ability to make decisions that may not be popular or may be contrary to those in power over you but are for the greater good. It is the strength to make decisions that could have adverse consequences to you as an individual. It requires the ability to question others and stand behind principles even when it is inconvenient for you.*

© Jennifer C. Wolfe 2020
J. C. Wolfe, *Disruption in the Boardroom*, https://doi.org/10.1007/978-1-4842-6159-0_2

As boards embrace change in the years ahead, they face a daunting enemy: the status quo. The silo mentality that feeds off of the status quo has permeated corporations for decades. In my first book written ten years ago, *Brand Rewired*, I interviewed executives from Fortune 100 companies about how to overcome the silo effect in innovation. One of my more memorable interviews was with Bob Wehling who started at Procter & Gamble in 1960 and retired in 1994 as Global Marketing Officer. He had particularly good insight into this issue having worked through many decades in the "Old Rules."

> *We were very much structured in silos for many years, as were most other businesses. During that time, the relationships we formed outside of our "silos" or departments was primarily up to us. But I think the people who were really successful understood the importance of reaching outside their department. Instinctively, I always understood that by working as a team we would get our work done better and faster. Those relationships, though, were largely up to us in the earlier days. We had to reach out and form the relationships with other departments, but I always found that's what brought the most success. Now there is more being done to facilitate and encourage those types of relationships and that's a really positive thing for companies and for consumers.*

We discussed at length the unfortunate reality of status quo thinking and silo mentalities that remained alive and well in many organizations today. When we look at companies that missed a change, such as Blockbuster or Sears or so many other now-defunct organizations, there is always a root cause problem that allowed the status quo to survive.

Where "New Rule" companies thrived was in setting a new culture and a new tone, but as they mature, they, too, run into the problem of managing the status quo. The reality is, if you reach the top of an organization, you might not want anything to change. Most of us inherently are working toward some goal: retirement, a next job or promotion, move to another company, or perhaps leaving some type of legacy. Whatever your goal, if you are successful you are usually laser focused on accomplishing it. This focus can leave your blinders on to what's coming at you from the sides.

It also means that senior leaders in organizations are not likely to embrace information that disrupts their path to achieving their goals. We are all human and all driven by some type of incentive. It could be money, flexibility in scheduling, travel, opportunities for exciting work, power over others, or feeling that your work makes a difference. Whatever incentives are put in place, however, will create the status quo. That's the thing about human nature – it is surprisingly consistent.

Most companies, particularly large ones, have a fundamental building block to incent employees by meeting budgets and completing road maps to achieve certain goals. This makes sense; it's a way to track and measure how you are doing. But when road maps take multiple years to execute, it leaves a lot of room for error as things change more rapidly than they ever have before. How do you create incentives to adapt to change? Companies of all sizes were forced to adapt when the 2020 Coronavirus Pandemic shut down business around the world and ordered individuals to stay in their home. Some companies adapted and even thrived with a new set of demands from consumers and businesses. Others were not able to move quickly enough or did not have the financial resources to weather the storm. We were all forced to adapt. As we return to work and some type of transition to "new normal" however, will the status quo return? What incentives will be in place?

If the incentives aren't right for senior leaders, the incentives will trickle down through the organization and create a culture that doesn't embrace change or disruption to existing plans. It can also mean leaders don't seek out multiple points of view and begin to exist in an echo chamber of similar ideas. We saw this play out in historical accounts of Blockbuster and Kodak. This is where real disruption is missed. As companies recover from the forced disruption of the 2020 Coronavirus Pandemic, other disruption still looms.

When leaders are avoiding risk to maintain their current success, the outcome is that subordinates will only report up new ideas or raise concerns when it serves the stated goal. It means there is a roadblock to new information, and ideas or concerns about the future may not be heard. When talented younger people don't feel they can make a meaningful contribution and are not heard, they will leave. Culture makes a difference in attracting and retaining talent. As a board, how are you creating a culture that incents and allows for disruption as the new normal? Do you have benchmarks where a strategy is reevaluated? Do you allow for a road map to be abandoned when new information suggest that is the right approach and still give the executives a bonus if they are making smart decisions for the future?

Incentives in the next decade may not follow the same patterns of the last two decades. Incentives need to allow for change and adaptation and reward critical thinking vs. just following a road map or hitting a top line number. Incentives need to address the continual state of disruption and the ability to recognize signals of change. As you look at incentives to adapt to disruption, make sure you clearly see the signals of business model shifts and not just the latest technology or tool.

Disruption Disguised

Disruption can take you by surprise if you aren't looking at the right issues. Amazon was once an online bookseller. As they emerged as the leader in the new era of ecommerce, other retailers began to pay attention. Many retailers flocked to copy their "ecommerce platform," but they missed what was actually happening. Amazon was really building a business model as a data and logistics company. This was what allowed them to migrate into new industries. Consider what businesses they are in now:

- Commercial distribution
- Home distribution/delivery
- Warehouse/sourcing solutions
- Entertainment network
- Cloud, software, and business solutions
- Grocer, retailer
- Data aggregator
- Clothing lines
- Pharmaceuticals
- Banks and financial services
- The Internet of things in the home – Alexa voice-based search and integration with other products

They are disrupting not just one industry but across sectors. While many retailers reacted to try to build the same ecommerce platform that powered Amazon, some missed the real shift that was occurring. Amazon was really mastering how to leverage data and then build the logistics machine to deliver anything – Alexa voice-based search, two-day delivery of almost anything, and award winning content on a streaming platform, to name just a few. They have built out a fleet of planes, helped their employees set up delivery companies, and built manufacturing facilities to make the products their data identifies as most profitable. While Amazon focused on building the engine that could transform them into any industry, the big retailers stayed focused on their road map to build an ecommerce platform. All the while, traditional retailers failed to see the data industry forming around them.

And then retailers woke up and suddenly decided they needed to hire data scientists and start tapping into data. But for many, if they don't change the culture, it won't matter. They won't be able to retain the talent they need when they don't allow innovative voices to be heard or take too long to adapt. The young data scientists are not going to stay in a company that doesn't really listen to the data.

In the boardroom, look for signs of status quo culture or that you are chasing the wrong disruptive force.

Signals of Status Quo Culture

How do you know if you have a status quo culture? Using the Amazon example, let's take a look at Kroger, Macy's, and Target, all companies hit hard by Amazon's emergence and the shift to online purchase. First, let's look at public comments from their respective CEOs about innovation:

Kroger CEO Rodney McMullen said in a WSJ article, Fall, 2019:

> Kroger must "step up our game. What we find is there's a lag between when you make those improvements and when the customer starts rewarding you with their checkbook."

Macy's CEO, Terry Lundgren, said at a retail conference in 2016:

> I think they're [Amazon] going to have an interesting challenge to start in getting all those returns back from online. . . We have stores, and consumers are going to return, particularly when they buy apparel online.

Walmart CEO, Doug McMillon, said in 2019 HBR interview:

> The whole point of such experimentation is to challenge the metabolism of the staid retailer and learn to 'fail fast' in pursuit of innovation that's a new concept in the culture of Walmart, where failure in general had never been an option, much less a desired outcome. We know there's a good chance it won't work, and that's okay, we'll learn stuff.

Target CEO, Brian Cornell, talked about how he actually rolled back some of their innovation projects in 2017 at Fortune's Brainstorm Tech Conference:

> Too many of Target's innovation ideas were drifting out into another universe. We had to reign them back in and say innovation has to first start with what is our guest expecting from target and how does it help our core enterprise.

Amazon's CEO, Jeff Bezos, said at a company meeting in 2018:

> One day, Amazon will fail, but our job is to delay it as long as possible.

From reading these quotes of CEOs, which company do you think has created a culture of disruption and innovation and is in synch with what customers are actually experiencing, ready to look at new ideas and ready to allow failure if it moves the company forward or to course correct if new information is presented? This is where boards can make a difference. Help your CEO embrace a culture of change, allow for new directions when necessary, support disruption, and create the environment to allow incentives to change.

Another way to see that if the status quo is at work is by looking at their patent portfolio. This is an indicator because it reflects the investment internally into new digital innovations as assets of the company. Table 2-1 compares the size of the current patent portfolio for Amazon, Macy's, Kroger, Walmart, and Target.

Table 2-1. US Patents Issued as of May 1, 2020

Company	Patents
Amazon	12,422
Macy's	4
Kroger	33
Walmart	1,113
Target	1,271

Patents are an important indicator of how a company values protecting the innovative ideas they are building. It is also indicative of the culture that exists. For most rank and file employees working in technology, data, and innovation, earning the title of "inventor" is career changing. Many brag about how many patents they have. Companies that don't build this culture will not be able to retain talented people in technology. I've helped companies build patent portfolios from nothing to competitive advantage, and when I do, I focused heavily on the culture as a centerpiece to success. It takes years to build even a small portfolio of 10 or 20 patents, so when you see Amazon out over 12,000 or Target above 1200 and Walmart creeping in, you know they have really course corrected internally. They have created a culture of innovation.

I've seen firsthand senior executives receive reports of how far ahead their competitors are in building a patent portfolio only to say that it doesn't matter, and they have other priorities. They receive this information that shows they are not on par with competitors and that other industry players are outperforming them, and instead of saying "what should we do about it," they refocus back on old goals that will be obsolete by the time they are finished. If you are on the board of a company without a patent portfolio, have you asked how you compare to your competitors? Not that patents are the only indicator of innovation, but in today's digital world, every company is a technology company. Most digital technology is patentable and companies competing in a global environment will take measures to protect what they invest in developing. This creates a strategic intelligence tool to help board members measure the culture of their organization against others as one metric.

The reality is, retailers don't have to chase after Amazon's patent portfolio to be successful, but they do need to understand it and be armed with the right information to make smart and strategic choices about how they will blend the fundamentals of profitability with an innovative culture understanding future trends. Patent analytics is a valuable tool for directors to have a key understanding of how your company compares to others. There is a way to do both, but the boardroom and status quo of leadership will have to be disrupted first.

None of this is exactly surprising. There have been studies for generations about the dangers of group think and how easily corporate leaders and boards can fall into that trap. In the seminal work on the subject, *Groupthink*,[1] Irving Janis says cohesive teams don't just emphasize collegiality in ways that suppress dissent. He also says cohesive teams: "dehumanize the enemy and think it is incompetent and limit the number of alternatives they will consider. They create mind guards who stomp out dissent."

Peter Drucker wrote in the *Effective Executive*[2] that "decisions of the kind the executive has to make are not made well by acclamation. They are made well only if based on conflicting views, the dialogue between different points of view, the choice between different judgments."

The lesson here is that if you maintain a status quo culture, don't embrace the ideologies of innovation, creation, and protecting what you build, you will not attract, retain, and create a culture that can adapt. The new models of business will blend old-school profitability standards and responsibility with new school innovative culture and thinking. To do so means that you must disrupt the boardroom and have the moral courage to question old-school status quo ways of doing things, particularly when it comes to culture and setting the right tone at the top.

If you maintain a status quo culture in your organization, you could have a crystal ball that told the future, and you wouldn't be able to execute on it because the culture won't accept a new reality and instead maintain the existing approach to doing business.

As you seek to understand how your company compares to competitors and whether or not you have a status quo culture that is limiting your ability to adapt in a disruptive world, consider the following sources:

- Analyze what your CEO says publicly and at trade conferences compared to the CEOs of competitors. Put them side by side for discussion in the boardroom.

- Compare your patent portfolio with that of competitors.

- Conduct a 360 review of people in your research and development and sales organization; find out what they think about how the company compares to competitors.

---

[1] Wadsworth, 1982.
[2] HarperCollins, 1967.

Also, watch for red flags in your organization. If you see any of the following, plan to discuss the status quo at your board meeting:

- Overly focused on technology adoption and deployment vs. problem-solving future customer needs.
- No shared vision of the future.
- Overuse of acronyms or jargon vs. defining what business you are in and how this aligns with long-term objectives.
- Too much focus on preserving corporate assets or values vs. a mindset of embracing the future and change.
- Not willing to abandon plans or thinking even when presented with new information that contradicts assumptions.
- Too much of the "not invented here syndrome" (meaning if they didn't think of the idea, then it is not a good idea)
- Education is too focused on hype vs. real implications (pros and cons).
- Too much reactive approaches to technology vs. thinking critically about the future.
- Lack of intellectual curiosity by management or fellow board members – ideas are fixed.
- Senior leaders delegate tech initiatives to middle management – not staying hands on.
- Incentives do not reward innovative thinking but status quo culture.
- If the board's knowledge is not sufficient, even if the tough questions are asked, directors may not be able to deliver true insight or perceive inconsistencies in management's responses.

Conclusion

If your board has a lack of diversity of thought (in addition to diversity of race, gender), it can create an echo chamber, and without challenge or incentives to respond to disruption, whatever is happening in your organization will perpetuate itself.

Unless we have moral courage to question ourselves, our leaders, and those who work for us and challenge the status quo on a continual basis, we will eventually be out of business. The 2020 Coronavirus Pandemic disrupted companies without warning and without giving most companies a choice to react. Most companies and boards simply had to respond with a disruption to the status quo. For many companies, that is likely a good thing and the question remains if they will revert back to old patterns when the crisis averts. Technological shifts and business model disruptions typically occur more subtly and without government mandates or shutdowns. Many of those trends that were already underway will be amplified; others will slow because of the enormous disruption of the global shutdown. The aftermath of the global pandemic and the ability to reflect upon how the company responded to the crisis and how it can be prepared for other disruptions is an important wake-up call.

Boards, in particular, in the role of oversight, need to be mindful and watchful if the status quo culture is impeding strategic thinking. If the members of the board don't probe and question to senior executives to avoid status quo thinking, no one else inside the organization will.

Discussion Questions for the Boardroom

1. How do you know if you have a status quo culture?

2. Do you allow incentives to change if new information is presented?

3. Do you talk to people working in your innovative groups or technology-focused groups to understand what motivates them?

4. Do you continually question what business you are in and what companies might move into your space (i.e., is Amazon coming for you)?

5. Do you ever hear executives dismiss ideas that come from other companies?

6. Do you know how many patents your company has vs. competitors?

7. Do you ever ask for a macro analysis of what type of things your company is patenting vs. what competitors are doing?

   a. You might be surprised at the results.

8. Do you follow your CEO and c-suite executives on social media?

   a. What does your CEO say about innovation, culture, and status quo?

9. Do you monitor what employees are saying on social media?

10. Do you check reviews on Glassdoor.com to see what employees leaving your company have to say about the culture?

Disruption and Digital Trends for the Next Decade

What you need to know in the boardroom about what's coming in layman's terms.

In this chapter, we'll talk about **discipline for continuous learning**. Invest the time, money, and resources to read, go to conferences, ask questions even if you fear you may be discovered for not understanding the subject, and learn about new technologies, new generations of thinking, and what's actually working or not working in your organization.

To be prepared for the disruption coming in the boardroom, we all need to invest in continuous learning. Most board directors were previously a CFO, CEO, or a President of a similarly sized organization to the company on which they serve. Most have been out of active operational roles for 5–10 years. There's nothing inherently wrong with this model; these individuals have

© Jennifer C. Wolfe 2020

J. C. Wolfe, *Disruption in the Boardroom*, https://doi.org/10.1007/978-1-4842-6159-0_3

experience and wisdom to offer sage counsel to the company. But it also means that when they were in operating roles, they weren't dealing with many of these disruptive issues. Without continuous learning and exposure to multiple points of view about future trends, there is no way for a director to understand the new technology, new vulnerabilities, or how these trends could disrupt your business. You have to start with a basic understanding of the technology and be open to challenging your assumptions about business models and future behavior. In this chapter, I will focus on disruptive and technology trends for the next decade.

It's important to think about not just one or two trends or one or two new technologies, but the intersection of how all of these changes will impact how we live and work as a society. Whether you build it, buy it, or license it, these technologies and trends will impact your company and how you operate it. However, you approach it, it will impact your workforce, and this is where you have to begin.

I've provided here a snapshot of a few of the big disruptive trends and what I think are worth watching at a broad level. There are many different ways to frame this or organize the information. You might not agree with mine, and that's okay. Take it for what it is – a viewpoint on trends that could impact the future and a starting point for your own analysis and discussion in the boardroom. In Chapter 7, I provide a framework to discuss these issues in the boardroom and pinpoint what could impact your organization. All of these trends were shifts I was watching before the 2020 Coronavirus Pandemic. I've added commentary to how they may be stalled or amplified as a result of the shutdown of the global economy. All of the trends identified here are based upon research cited in the "References" section of the book for further reading. I also provide my trend forecasting methodology in the "Appendix" section of this chapter along with an overview of the underlying technologies referenced.

Voice-Based Search Tied to Artificial Intelligence and the Internet of Things

Why this is a trend. We are migrating to a point where our search will fully convert from typing into a computer or a device to talking or giving verbal commands. If you're comfortable interacting with Siri or Alexa, you may already be there, but the tipping point is coming for everyone soon. Voice recognition software is getting better and better. As it connects to full functioning artificial intelligence (AI) and learns from its interactions with you, it will be able to better understand you and deliver what you want without requiring you to type anything. Likewise, AI will connect to all the things in our life: our car, our thermostat, refrigerator, perhaps the house itself, even your bed at night could become a thing connected to the Internet responding to your voice commands with sensors to help you achieve restful sleep and better health. Some important areas of artificial intelligence connected to devices to consider:

- Manufacturing: AI will allow data insights to enhance safety, reduce costs, and yield better response.

- Retail: AI will drive recommendations, improve inventory, and supply chain.

- Health care: From shorter wait times to improved patient outcomes, AI will improve the ability to recognize symptoms and seek treatment. In the aftermath of the pandemic, it seems likely AI will be used to track how a virus spreads and where it could be going.

- Financial services: AI will help data security, accounting practices, and smarter decision making about money.

- Government: AI will improve speed and quality of services.

- Education: Digitized textbooks will help virtual tutors assist students, and facial analysis will predict emotions to determine who's struggling or bored.

- Farming: AI will help farmers better predict what's coming, what to plant, and when to water and reduce waste.

- Transportation: AI could power automobiles, planes, trains, and other forms of transportation to be developed.

- Other unique applications include better management of tracking endangered species, composing music, and predicting depressed individuals in a school or work environment, among many other uses across industries. All of which, of course, come with potentially bad consequences if the AI or the IOT it is connected to gets it wrong.

An important point   Artificial intelligence is a term that has morphed in meaning. Originally, it meant deep machine learning, meaning the software or computer could continue to learn based upon inputs and interactions and build upon the original code. It has evolved to mean data-based algorithms or almost anything using data inputs. It's evolved because every company wants to say it uses artificial intelligence, so the standard was lowered. The Bloomberg Intelligence economist Michael McDonough tracked mentions of artificial intelligence in earnings call transcripts, noting a huge uptick in the last two years. For this reason, many reports and accounts of AI are skewed, and differing viewpoints emerge on what is actually AI vs. just using data in an automated manner.

What I'm watching. I'm watching closely which companies will win the race as the voice recognition software of choice. Whichever company captures the largest market share with their technology will dominate how we search the Internet in the future and capture all of that data. Every time you use their technology, they will track it. It concerns me that only a few companies could dominate all of search in the future. We've already seen the dangers of companies like Amazon, Facebook, or Google becoming the central source of data on all of us. Many companies are partnering with Amazon to integrate Alexa into their products. For example, Kohler has rolled out bathroom products like showers, bathtubs, toilets, and even mirrors that are connected to the Internet and respond to voice commands with Alexa software. If they can now penetrate your private bathroom in your home to know what you read or what music or information you want at your most private of moments, that is cause for concern. Some say the conveniences are worth it. If you can reorder toilet paper at the moment you know you need it and Amazon delivers it in two hours, that certainly has some convenience factor. But if there's a camera in the mirror, what's to prevent it from being hacked and used against you. There are also startups I am watching who offer private-label voice recognition so that if Kohler wanted to have its own voice recognition software, it could do so. The challenge will become, if it's not linked to Amazon, how do you add all of the functionality? This is the conundrum we are now in. Directors need to think carefully about how they partner with other technology companies. It may give a leg up in the short term but in the long term could marry you up with a partner who has all the power.

The annual Consumer Electronics Show showcases startups in technology including voice recognition technology. Many companies are also now partnering with local incubators to tap into new ideas and technologies. Consider alternatives to big tech as you embrace these big new trends like voice recognition tied to artificial intelligence.

Drones

Why this is a trend. Drone technology is well developed from military applications to personal "joy riding" around the neighborhood. Amazon is seeking to utilize drone technology for same-day delivery or reaching hard to get to rural places where a robotic drone flown remotely by an operator can drop off packages. The theory is this reduces costs by eliminating trucks and drivers to go to those remote places. It eliminates delivery vehicles on the road for same-day delivery in urban areas. While the FAA has approved drones for commercial use in some areas, there remain many questions to be answered by federal and local governments. I was recently at a hotel in Florida and someone in a room above me was flying a drone around. The drone peered into my hotel room, so I called the manager and he brought it to a stop. I was concerned about the drone peering in the room with a camera. It may have been completely innocent or perhaps not. But what will we find acceptable on a personal level? On a much more dangerous level, Gatwick Airport in London, December 2018, was brought to a halt for more than 33 hours impacting more than 140,000 passengers as someone or some group dangerously flew drones up into the air traffic path. The danger with commercial air traffic is without a doubt one of the greatest to consider in the questions about drones.

- How many drones could we have flying around?
- Who is licensed to fly them?
- What happens to any element of privacy?
- What about bad guys stealing our stuff from the drone?
- What about hacking the drone to deliver packages somewhere else or crash into a car driving 70 mph on the highway?
- What about turning the drone into a weapon?
- What happens when a misdirected drone causes a plane crash?

During the 2020 Coronavirus Pandemic, many local governments considered using drones to track groups assembling against local ordinances or to track the health of individuals. Is that a violation of our privacy rights? The debate about privacy over public health is just beginning.

What I'm watching. I'm closely watching regulatory discussions of drone technology. This is really the pivotal issue. This is a Pandora's box if it is allowed to be opened. Much like social media is out there and can't be put back in the box. We have two generations of young people whose mental health has been affected by the negative impacts of social media. If drones are not carefully regulated outside of specific use cases (like military or rural applications), it could be a slippery slope to Orwellian privacy concerns. It exacerbates the concerns we already have about a few companies possessing too much information about us. I'm also looking at the positives of drone technology, aiding in law enforcement, emergency response, disaster relief, conservation efforts, health care, agriculture, and waste management. The need for drone technology is real, but efforts to curtail bad actors or just hazardous juvenile behavior are a policy struggle for the future.

Continue to watch the startups that innovate and the policy makers who will make it safe. There are a number of sources that aggregate this data including the Alliance for Drone Innovation and the Drone Innovators Network at the World Economic Forum, among others.

Driverless Cars

Why this is a trend. The technology for driverless cars was actually invented in the 1960s at Ohio State University. In 1969, IEEE spectrum published an article entitled "The Electronic Highway" by two engineers from Ohio State, Robert Fenton and Karl Olson. The technology has come a long way with test cars on the roads for Google, Uber, Tesla, and even the traditional automakers for many years. Google's Waymo has logged the greatest number of hours. We know the technology is here and it works, but there are still some challenges to be solved. The next decade will see much of the regulatory work and infrastructure work needed to safely allow automated vehicles merge in with traditional cars driven by humans. While many tout the benefit of reduced fatalities by computers driving cars, the emerging industry remains plagued with stories of safety drivers failing to do their job and humans killed by a car that doesn't read a sensor or isn't familiar with a situation. If you've ever driven your car in the snow where many of the auto functions are on (like lane assist that keeps your car centered in the lane, etc.), you know that sensors don't always work in bad weather. This is why the majority of the test programs are in California or Arizona where it is primarily sunny and doesn't get below freezing. And, for all that electric cars can do, across manufacturers, 40% of their range is reduced in extremely cold weather, according to AAA. There is still some technology development needed to address changes in environment at a cost that consumers can afford. The proponents of automated vehicles cite that the trucking industry could be revolutionized. But even those tests determine a human driver would still be needed in congested urban areas and that the primary benefits are on long-haul drives with primarily straight roadways. Certainly, we are headed in this direction, but opportunities exist in helping to solve the problems in the last mile.

What I'm watching. I'm excited about the prospect of automated vehicles. The ability of a vehicle to take over in bumper-to-bumper traffic or on a long-haul straight shot is appealing. But, I'm more interested right now in how some key questions are answered.

- What happens to all of the traditional cars?
- Could the government force you to give up your car?
- How much data and power will big tech have when they own the cars that drive us around?
- What happens when a foreign state could take over all of our cars or you accidentally click on a phishing email connected to your car while driving?
- What level of privacy will remain if one company now has access to all of this information about you or has a camera on you while you are in your own car?

- How many years will it take for people to give up their cars where drivers and robots occupy the roads together?

- Will this give the "have nots" more cost-effective access to transportation, or will it further divide those who can afford a driverless car vs. those who cannot?

- Could it further trap the poor into using technology owned by a limited few companies where their data is their currency?

- Will police vehicles be unmanned with computers making decisions?

- What companies will power the artificial intelligence?

- What if the goal of reducing traffic accidents doesn't change because computers make mistakes, too, or don't have all of the variables programmed in?

- If local municipalities rely on a certain amount of traffic ticket violations for its budget, how will that get replaced if robots don't make mistakes?

There are many questions to be answered to realize the potential of automated vehicles. In those questions are tremendous opportunities, as well as challenges.

New Energy Sources

Why this is a trend. At Davos 2020, the annual World Economic Forum, climate change and reducing carbon emissions was front and center as the issue of the day for corporations and intellectual thought leaders. I realize that there are diverging views on the timing of climate change and some groups that don't believe it is occurring at all. I try not to be political in my research or advisory work with boards of directors because all viewpoints need to be heard and understood. Wherever you are in your personal beliefs on climate change, the one generally accepted business principle is that there is now a demand for companies to take steps to limit carbon emissions and find alternative energy sources. Microsoft announced at Davos 2020 that it would erase its carbon footprint with its future strategies to include a $1 billion innovation fund to develop carbon removal technology and focus on cleaning carbon from the atmosphere. Of course, just days later, they fired up diesel generators when the power went out at one of its facilities. Across industries, there will clearly continue to be a debate about how to balance cost-effective energy needs in a modern world with stewardship of our planet for future generations.

What I'm watching. The Bill and Melinda Gates Foundation is continuing to investigate how to safely use alternative sources of power, including nuclear power as just such a solution. Their investment in TerraPower has focused on solving that problem but also faced setbacks. Their work to find solutions, wherever they may be, could ultimately mean that families can afford to buy efficient energy homes without relying on traditional energy sources. Air, wind, solar, biomass, geothermal, and biofuels are all also in the mix, but widespread accessibility to the average consumer is still developing. There's no question this is a polarizing and emotional topic, particularly for many Millennials and Gen Z who believe that the older generations are putting their future in jeopardy. Power and energy are a central factor to all businesses and to our very way of life. It's clearly a marketing advantage to show how you are environmentally savvy (see more in Chapter 6 about the latest environmental and social governance trends), but there is also a balancing act of practicality. How do you do what Microsoft is doing (i.e., power your company effectively while also delivering on promises for environmental stewardship)?

Changes in the Housing Market

Why this is a trend. New home sales in 2019 reached the highest numbers since 2007, and existing home sales were up nationwide in 2019 according to the National Association of Home Builders. As millennials finally begin to reach the age and stage of their life where they are getting married, making a better salary, and having kids, they are realizing they can't afford to live in urban centers. Accordingly, they are migrating out of big expensive cities and flocking to places like Boise, Idaho; Raleigh-Durham, North Carolina; Louisville, Kentucky; Salt Lake City, Utah; Memphis and Nashville, Tennessee; Houston, Texas; Detroit, Michigan; Indianapolis, Indiana; and Columbus, Ohio; to name just a few. They find new jobs and more affordable housing to begin their "adult" life.

As they move, they are no longer looking for the "big home" that was a status symbol to Boomer and Gen Xers, but rather something smaller and more affordable in a nice community that gives them access to the "urban" environment they like without the price tag. Older generations are also leaving high tax states because of the change in tax laws that now limits the federal deduction of local taxes. Couple all of this with the reality that new homes will need to tap into new energy sources (California already requires new homes to have solar panels) and changing technology capabilities for enabled smart homes, and we are poised to see tremendous growth and change in the housing market in the years ahead. This leaves an inventory of many old homes that may no longer be wanted or need complete refurbishment. In the aftermath of the 2020 Coronavirus Pandemic, its likely many living in urban areas may also question if that is the best place to live in the future.

As work shifts to remote work vs. in-office work as a result, the opportunity for many to leave densely populated environments may result in further expansion of new housing to meet that demand.

What I'm watching. I'm closely watching how the construction industry will leverage robotics and increased automation to deliver on the demands of the future. I'm also looking to corporations that recognize the migration out of big cities and how they will create "corporate communities" to deliver affordable housing with a community-driven culture to meet the needs of Millennial and Gen Z workers. In the vein of "Levittown" of the 1960s, the idea of smaller affordable homes with a community approach will continue to expand. I'm also watching how the vacation rental regulations are changing. We could see many areas that were once resident-driven communities evolve as vacationer havens. In costly urban areas, many homeowners may opt for their place to become an investment opportunity while moving to greener pastures that are more cost-effective. We can also expect to see styles and designs of homes evolve as the need for technology integrated into the home expands. Finally, I am watching how smaller communities outside of big urban centers create land trusts or opportunity zones to attract investors – this could give real estate investors new incentives as well as build communities in smaller markets looking to grow.

5G, Fiber Optic, and Speed

Why this is a trend. Speed is the contingency for the new world order. Every trend identified here in this chapter requires fast Internet access. For an entire population to be living their life connected to things and devices powered by artificial intelligence and streaming news, content, and information, and navigating autonomous vehicles, we will need a faster Internet connection. Most of the big telecom companies have rolled out some form of 5G, but the technology is not quite refined like it seems on the ads you may see. There are still glitches, limited range, and a lot of infrastructure to roll this out of big urban areas. The next decade will see this technology refinement and infrastructure development. On the flip slide, fiber optic cable also provides the type of speed that will be needed. Today, there's only about 25% of the United States powered by fiber optic cable. Google's Fiber company is one of the fastest growing, but it's costly to install fiber to homes and businesses.

What I'm watching. With threats of net neutrality limiting what the Internet service providers (ISPs) can charge, this means that the regulatory landscape impacts investment decisions. All businesses and consumers will need higher-speed Internet in the future. Net neutrality is a double-edged sword. It could mean that a few companies are regulated or supported by the government to provide cost-effective high-speed access equally. On the flip side, if there is regulation without subsidies, it means the Internet service providers (ISPs) lack financial incentive to provide high-speed access. Without net neutrality, the ISPs have the right to choose to block sites, speed up or slow down service to customers based upon what level of service they pay for and how much data they use, or even provide fast lanes directly to the streaming services. This gives them the financial incentive for the important infrastructure development. This is an important regulatory debate that has two good arguments on each side. Either way, I am carefully watching the investment being made by the big telecom and ISP providers to see what they will do in the future. In the aftermath of the 2020 Coronavirus Pandemic, it is unquestionable that speed of Internet access will be demanded by all. How government regulation of this industry impacts innovation and speed to market will be important to watch closely.

Global Internet Decentralization

Why this is a trend. The Internet has never been free and open everywhere. Since its inception, many parts of the world like China, Russia, and the Middle East censor most aspects of the Internet. Only in the United States, Canada, and most of Europe is the Internet truly open and available. In Europe, General Data Protection Regulation (GDPR), implemented beginning May 2018, meant that companies doing business on the Internet had to comply with certain costly legal requirements in order to do business with their citizens, ostensibly creating a barrier or wall to their Internet. It has long been thought that the existing Internet infrastructure may become decentralized or bifurcated. Google's founder, Eric Schmidt, has posited that the Internet will splinter, and we will see a different connection in different parts of the world. The implications are profound if the World Wide Web suddenly has borders and tariffs to be paid to cross those borders. Many argue that has already happened. With new technologies like blockchain (as a means of connecting computers together), it's possible we could see a migration to a new way of connecting everyone – with the ripple effect into the "smart everything" world into which we are evolving that has big questions on when, how, and what does it mean.

What I'm watching. I'm closely watching the implementation and enforcement of GDPR in Europe. It's likely that the United States will also enact some legislation to protect privacy and hold businesses more accountable for business conducted online. Within the United States, some states, like California, are already doing just that. As we end up with a complex maze of rules to follow, it complicates how digital business is managed and how companies plan for the future. And it creates the opening for a new Internet or way of connecting everything to form. As that happens, the rules of the road could change. I'm also watching the fines charged against tech companies. For example, Google was fined $1.7 billion for its unfair advertising practices in Europe and has subsequently faced claims upward of $9 billion for violations of antitrust laws. Facebook could face up to $1.63 billion in fines over a data breach violating the new GDPR, and Amazon is under investigation. I also continue to watch how Internet policy is developed globally and whether "new webs" form. If that starts to happen, companies need to pay attention quickly and make smart decisions about its entire Internet infrastructure.

Tech Trust Busting and Data Privacy

Why this is a trend. In the last couple of years, as leaders from Facebook, Google, Amazon, Twitter, and Apple have been invited to Capitol Hill to help legislators understand their business model, the great awakening has occurred. Consumers and lawmakers alike now realize that all of these "free" platforms come at a cost – privacy. As cameras and voice-activated devices infiltrate every facet of our daily life, the ease of invading privacy is no longer science fiction. Hackers can tap into your Nest cameras, Ring cameras, Zoom meetings, and devices to peer into your private life. Combined with the vast amount of data just a handful of companies possess and their ability to favor their own sales channels and advertising over others, expect to see an increase in antitrust investigations and data privacy legislation. In a post-pandemic era, there are many who believe that these issues will be dismissed in favor of public health. The technology already exists to track and trace people, but does that violate constitutional rights of citizens? Does that infringe on privacy in a way that is not acceptable? In my interviews with board members on this issue, I've found that those located in hard-hit areas like New York City say that for the greater good, we all have to give up our privacy rights. Others, however, maintain that we can't allow this to occur or further liberties will be eroded. Balancing technology with privacy rights and varying degrees of intrusion for what some view as a greater good or convenience will continue to be a policy debate in the future.

What I'm watching. No matter which political party is in power, there will be scrutiny of the big five: Google, Amazon, Facebook, Apple, and Twitter, as well as others. Despite political polarization, this scrutiny is largely bipartisan and is one voters want addressed. I'm watching pending legislation and investigations by agencies into these companies and how big tech CEOs are positioning themselves for what's coming and alternative strategies forward. I'm also watching how privacy will become an industry. Consumers may pay a service provider to help them monitor and protect their privacy, particularly as laws evolve with a "right to be forgotten." Likewise, as businesses may need help complying with all of these laws, expect to see a cottage industry form around privacy. If a post-pandemic era includes significant surveillance or monitoring, particularly related to travel and gatherings, then expect to see increasing regulation of how that information is used. The cottage industry to help individuals protect their privacy will emerge stronger than ever.

Oversight of Artificial Intelligence and Robotics

Why this is a trend. In the next decade, alongside privacy as an industry, the concept of oversight of artificial intelligence and robotics will also become an industry unto itself. It's a trend because the dangers of bias in artificial intelligence are well accepted. The CEO of Google, Sundar Pichai, in a January 20, 2020, Forbes article cited the need for regulation. Bias forms in multiple ways in artificial intelligence. Amazon was using AI to help recruit for its tech teams. It used data sets from who had been successful in the past. That data set was comprised almost entirely of men. Accordingly, the AI used data that favored men and was biased (unintentionally) against women. If the data going in has a bias, the data going out will share the bias. Likewise, if AI doesn't have all the information it needs or encounters a new situation, it may not perform as we would like. Many of the self-driving car accidents have been a result of AI that didn't know what it was encountering combined with sensors delivering inaccurate or incomplete information. The Boeing 737 Max jet crashes of 2019 have also been cited as potentially a combination of AI and sensors getting it wrong combined with humans unable to override it fast enough. Additionally, AI learns based upon interactions. Depending upon *who* is interacting with early AI, it could become biased by those individuals. As we integrate more AI and robotics into daily life, the need for some human oversight is clear. While regulation will be important to ensure responsibility is factored in, the opportunity for companies to create human oversight as a job or as a service will grow. It's hard to audit yourself. This is why outside "oversight" or watchdogs may be needed or regulated in the future.

What I'm watching. I'm closely watching the companies that are building AI such as Apple, Amazon, Microsoft, Google, Facebook, IBM, Intel, Salesforce, and others and how they propose to self-regulate. I'm also watching how the governments of the world begin to address this issue, as well as new companies forming to fill this gap. While it's commendable that the big tech companies are offering to self-regulate before there is an "Enron" situation or a "Cambridge Analytica" (this is the company that exploited Facebook's lax policies on data) moment, it's still concerning that such a few companies could house so much data and power. Typically, companies are not great at self-regulating. That's how we ended up with Enron. I'm watching closely how the regulatory environment changes. Directors should keep an eye on this, too, and continuously question how the company uses AI and robotics and how it is ensuring a bias or unintended consequence is not happening.

Virtual and Augmented Reality

Why this is a trend. The technology for virtual reality is almost where it needs to be to become more than just a game or a toy to something that truly transforms experiences. The potential to allow grander and more enriching experiences will impact health and wellness, travel and tourism, shopping and retail, as well as gaming and entertainment. Imagine for a moment that as you age and can no longer physically travel, you have regrets of never visiting the Sistine Chapel or hiking Machu Picchu, but you could visit a high-end 4D virtual reality center and spend the afternoon seeing, feeling, and hearing everything you might while actually there. Or, if you were wheelchair bound at a young age and wanted to know what it might feel like to walk the Great Wall of China. Or, if you can't afford to travel long distances or take the time off of work, but want to see the Northern Lights, all of this can be possible. Likewise, if you are living in a cold environment in the winter and could mediate for a half hour a day on a warm beach, might that change your physical and mental outlook? The possibilities are endless in improving the quality of life through this technology. If through augmented reality you can picture a new living room set or paint color in your house or try on that new dress or suit and then purchase it, it could transform what we want from our retailers. All of this technology exists but is not refined or cost-effectively available. That will likely change in the next decade. The 2020 Pandemic highlighted the need for such services and technology. In the aftermath, many people may no longer feel safe to travel in the way they did previously. And, after a lock down, the need to have a way to escape will become in high demand.

What I'm watching. I'm closely watching the rollout of new products and the level of technology. Facebook owns Oculus Rift, which is one of the best VR headsets available to consumers. There are many others and researchers at MIT seeking to use commercial-level VR combined with true 4D experiences. In fact, one study allows individuals to feel like they are a tree in a rainforest and know what it's like if a fire is coming toward you. In a combination of spiritual and awakening, the experience is transformative. As spas and hotels roll out virtual reality–based meditation rooms as a new form of recreation or escape at affordable prices, we will see a shift in global spending on travel. Likewise, health care could truly change if the mental state of a patient could be improved all from a hospital bed or at home. Directors in these industries should be thinking about how this could disrupt or complement your existing product offerings. It could also improve daily experiences for employees if they are able to take a "power trip" in the middle of the day to refresh and reenergize with a fresh perspective.

New Supply Chains and Management (Blockchain and Others)

Why this is a trend. Much of the innovative trends discussed here have largely had a consumer impact. Behind the scenes, the supply chain is being transformed. Blockchain as a new form of a database connecting an entire supply chain together could reduce costs and improve transparency. Industries like insurance, digital rights, financial services, food suppliers, trucking, and distribution, to name just a few, could be impacted. I wrote a book in 2018 entitled *Blockchain in the Boardroom*. If you want a full deep dive into what blockchain could do, check it out. For now, know that vertical industries investing in blockchain could see a disruptive force to their legacy systems. The rationale is that the blockchain database could be more secure, reduce costs and employees needed to manage transactions, and improve traceability within a supply chain. In the aftermath of the 2020 Coronavirus Pandemic, many blockchain researchers I know and talk to are looking at how blockchain could help with supply chain in the medical industry and food industry to solve problems faster when needed.

What I'm watching. I'm watching companies like Microsoft, IBM, Walmart, Bank of America, Fidelity, and Ernst & Young who are out in the forefront of development and test cases using blockchain. As they refine this technology, we will determine if blockchain will truly be transformative. The challenge for blockchain is that there are big legacy systems to overhaul and for it to work requires everyone in your supply chain to cooperate.

Back to Basics – The End of the Era of Unicorns

Why this is a trend. The tipping point is clearly coming even in Silicon Valley as venture capitalists begin to report a concern about the lack of profitability in even their most promising investments. As companies like Theranos and WeWork have turned out to be fraudulent, masquerading as a tech company with creative accounting to hide the reality and Unicorns like Uber, Airbnb, Snapchat, and so many others are still not turning a profit after nearly a decade in business, the market may no longer tolerate such a long and expensive lead time to basic business fundamentals with outsized valuations. While there will still be venture capital investment for scaled innovation, there will likely be greater scrutiny even for a charismatic CEO. While investors will still look for visionaries, they may temper the erratic behavior of a Founder-CEO sooner.

What I'm watching. I am carefully watching what big venture capitalists say at conferences and in interviews, as well as what is the word on the street from companies trying to raise money in a new climate. I'm carefully looking at the companies that remain teetering on the edge of profitability for another dot-com-like crisis where the irrational exuberance bubble eventually bursts, likely this decade. It could also impact the entire "sharing economy" model.

Automation Meets Infrastructure

Why this is a trend. For the transformative technology that exists (i.e., artificial intelligence, the Internet of things, driverless cars, drones, blockchain, and others) to translate into real changes in our life, infrastructure changes will be needed to scale the potential. For example, our roadways are not designed for automated cars interacting with humans. Urban areas were not built for 5G and fiber optic cable. Most buildings were designed and structured for last century technology instead of a virtual, augmented, or fully automated component to the workforce. With climate change driving a need for alternative energy in smart homes and smart office buildings, something's going to change in the next decade.

What I'm watching. I'm watching carefully the construction industry and how it is adapting to these new demands, as well as how and where fiber and 5G are being deployed. Which companies will provide the services needed to facilitate this change – there is opportunity there. I'm also carefully watching who is going to dominate the connection between artificial intelligence, the Internet of things, and voice-based search to create the standards that will follow us across our lives. Right now, this is Amazon, Microsoft, Facebook, Google, and Intel.

Supply Chain and the Return to Locally vs. Globally Sourced

Why this is a trend. Climate change pressure will go beyond how we use plastic or what car we drive into the very nature of how we deliver goods and services around the world. Combined with a desire to eat healthy, fresh locally grown goods, the demand for more locally sourced products and services will trickle throughout the supply chain. Referred to by consultants as "localization," this trend has been emerging over the last couple of years. Additionally, the need for more jobs in suburban and rural areas where the cost of living is more affordable for the average person will create new opportunities to produce and supply goods people need locally instead of on the other side of the world. While global commerce is certainly not going away, there will be an increased demand for alternatives to shipping goods across the world and supporting local businesses. In the aftermath of the 2020 Coronavirus Pandemic, sourcing goods from China will be carefully reevaluated by many companies. The need to source essential goods locally to expedite delivery time will increase as businesses reflect upon the impact of the 2020 Pandemic.

What I'm watching. I'm carefully watching changes in the agriculture and food production business to allow for production of food in new ways that can be grown and delivered locally reducing the carbon footprint and increasing nutritional value. Companies like Amazon are helping their employees begin distribution companies around the globe to better meet distribution channels with less long-haul trucks, cars, planes, and boats required. Of course, trade policies impact long-term strategy of businesses as they prepare for a potential future where cheap overseas labor may no longer be cheap. I'm also watching the companies that start building community-driven training programs or partner with universities to feed well-trained graduates into their companies to allow for the human capital needed on a more localized basis. I anticipate we will also see a shift in how medical equipment and supplies are sourced in the aftermath of the 2020 Coronavirus Pandemic. Governments and health-care systems alike will look for domestic sources of important equipment and set policies to drive that goal.

The Business of Health Care

Why this is a trend. The Baby Boomer population is aging with more health care available than ever in our history. They will live longer than any generation before them. Gen X, Millennials, and Gen Z will all live longer than previous generations. At the same time, the system that promises to pay retirees for their health care will eventually run out of money. The business of health care simply has to change or evolve. Additionally, artificial intelligence and robotics will disrupt hospital and medical care. The same issues that have already been addressed about privacy and oversight are amplified when it comes to our health because the unintended consequences can be life threatening. The concern for a cyberattack is also of greater concern. In the aftermath of the 2020 Coronavirus Pandemic, preparation of the health-care system for future viruses or pandemics will become part of the new normal for the business of health care.

What I'm watching. I don't expect this to be fixed in Washington D.C. in such a polarized environment anytime soon. I'm carefully looking at the entrepreneurial community and innovation labs from Fortune 500 to innovate new ways to help the health-care industry cut costs, improve security to avoid a catastrophe, utilize biometric and new tools to better deliver services, drive health and wellness from the start, and help make health care more affordable. Government will have to fix the end game solution of how it is all structured and reign in insurance and pharmaceutical companies, but in the meantime, look to the innovation of entrepreneurial companies and innovation labs to help solve the surrounding problems. Fast Company puts out annual lists of innovative companies by sector, including health care. This is a great source for tracking the companies that could change everything. I am also watching ethical issues about who owns your DNA and what can be done with it.

While many have flocked to companies like 23andMe or Ancestry to get a DNA test, many don't realize that those companies now own their DNA. This will likely get more attention in the future when policy makers determine who can own DNA and what they can do with it.

The Enron Moment in Cybersecurity

Why this is a trend. It is widely accepted among security experts that we will never be "safe" or free from cyber threats. In fact, many cite concerns that the big one is already planted in systems and just needs to be activated. Despite increased attention to this issue, as companies are facing so many threats and a bit of fatigue on the subject of cybersecurity, this one could get less attention at the time it is needed it the most. Much like how Enron awakened the public and government to the threats of self-dealing and lack of transparency in accounting practices, the same may be true in cybersecurity practices. I go deeper into cybersecurity in the next chapter.

What I'm watching. I'm closely watching how the Securities and Exchange Commission (SEC) is beginning to hold boards and corporations more accountable for their cyber readiness. I'm watching legislation that has been pending for several years to address this issue. I'm also watching closely which companies continue to source critical IT services from China, the Ukraine, and other hot spots for potential corruption or intrusion. See more in Chapter 4.

Digital Currency and the Future of Money

Why this is a trend. Bitcoin was just a teaser and is mired in controversy because of nefarious activity associated with cryptocurrency. But, new forms of trading a digital asset of value will be demanded as consumers seek alternate ways to participate in economic growth. Digital currency already exists in video game culture and many Internet-based ecosystems. The same concept exists for those who buy gold or art as an investment. It's not hard to see this translate into digital assets of new forms.

What I'm watching. I'm watching the big financial players and their patent portfolios carefully. This helps me understand what new tools they may deploy to create the infrastructure and credibility needed for digital assets to begin to replace traditional currency. I'm also closely watching the governments of the world as they will begin to regulate digital assets to provide some stability to the market. Finally, I'm watching Apple, Google, Facebook, and Amazon as they could most easily roll out and scale their own digital dollars. Further, peer-to-peer payment systems will also likely further develop.

Other Trends

These are just a few of the digital-driven disruptive tends I'm watching as we move deeper into the 2020s and beyond. The next decade is a big one. Unfortunately, it started with a global shutdown during the 2020 Coronavirus Pandemic. Many of these trends will be amplified as a result, few will stall. The disruption that is coming from these trends was thrust onto everyone during a shutdown, but as things return to normal, focus should be paid to how those trends will accelerate. We will see not just technological advances, but the changes in infrastructure and society required to move us out of the roaring 20s and into the next midcentury age. The companies that pay attention to the trends, set the right incentives for their workforce to adapt and change, and embrace a culture of continual change and improvement will survive and drive our future. The role of the board of directors in providing governance and oversight in this critical decade will change as everything around them does. I hope you will have the intellectual honesty to question old assumptions, see potential new future possibilities, have the moral courage to question management when needed, and offer the leadership we all will need from Corporate America.

There are, obviously, so many other areas to explore; I've selected for a quick overview the ones that have the most pervasive impact.

Other trends to be watching include the race to *space* including minisatellites and consumer travel of the future, as well as continued exploration of space. Like all of the other trends we've discussed, the question of how it will be governed and who will have control is pervasive.

Media and content, of course, has now evolved to the Streaming Wars. Integrating with 5G speed, the Internet of things, and the integration between gaming and entertainment and shopping will continue to be trends to watch, as well as consolidation of the streaming providers. Content will get easier to produce, but the distribution will become further consolidated putting a lot of power in the hands of a few.

Biometrics will continue to be a path to greater security balanced with privacy concerns. **Consumer goods** will also change as Millennials and Gen Z think differently about what they buy and what they value. The way people shop and interact will change. After the 2020 Coronavirus Pandemic, there was already a shift in what types of food and home goods people demanded. I'll cover more of this in Chapter 5.

To make sure everyone has some of the basics covered, I've outlined some important elements about the fundamental underlying technology to these trends in Appendix A.

Conclusion

Human behavior is surprisingly consistent even if the scenery and circumstances change. That's why all of these trends are about more than just technology – it's technology matched up with consumer behavior. In the next few chapters, we'll explore what's happening in cybersecurity and what vulnerabilities are created, as well as the societal shifts that are coming in consumer behavior and the future of work. All of these factors will create new challenges and shape the trends as they unfold. The challenges are opportunities for the businesses who can solve for them.

As you approach this broad topic of digital disruption in the next decade from the boardroom, be sure to not just understand the overarching trends, but consider the following key components:

Interconnectedness: None of these things will happen in isolation. Everything is interconnected. As you address the disruptive trends outlined in this chapter, leverage cross-functional teams who bring different perspectives. Build advisory teams outside of your organization who come from different points of view to ensure you aren't missing something. Too often, leaders surround themselves with others just like them – diversity of thought is the future of diversity and the only way to understand fully how these future trends impact you positively and negatively – it's opportunities and challenges equally considered.

Partnerships and strategic alignments: These will become essential to future business. No one business will be able to dominate all of the areas, so leveraging other businesses and strengths will become a key to future success. Carefully consider with whom you partner and how – it could mean the difference between obsolescence and survival.

Supply chain management: While this has always been an issue, developing a more streamlined supply chain and cultivating a supply chain with less risk will become increasingly important. While the past theory has been to squeeze everything you can out of a supply chain, a migration toward greater loyalty and partnership will likely be key as these trends engulf all industries.

Labs and hubs of innovation: You will not survive without investing in places internally where innovation can take place without an immediate return on investment. Not only do you need the creative and innovative ideas, but you need to attract and retain a workforce from future generations to survive. See more in Chapter 5 about the future of work but know that future generations want to feel connected to where they work and believe that what they are doing makes a difference. Creating spaces that invite innovative thinking and allow for idea development without an immediate financial return on investment will be critically important to all businesses. Additionally, consider programs that can help facilitate open innovation (meaning attracting innovative ideas from the outside). This can be through vendor relationships, as well as partnering with incubators and universities.

Mergers and acquisitions: Acquiring the technology or accelerating your growth in an area will always be an attractive option for scaling quickly or taking out a competitor early, but be cautious you don't destroy the culture that created whatever it is you are acquiring. In the last couple of decades, companies have gobbled up smaller players to remove them from the marketplace, but also, in many instances, lost what was making that company special. As you consider acquisitions, give careful attention to culture and identifying what has value beyond just technology or scale potential. Don't just pay a big consulting firm to do it and then check the box as you destroy the acquired company, think about what you are really acquiring and cultivate it.

Discussion Questions for the Boardroom

1. Do you partner with local universities or incubator hubs?

   a. How do you tap into startups and new technology?

2. Do you encourage open innovation in your company?

3. Should your company migrate to voice-based search? If so, how will it do that?

4. How will drones impact your company's services or employee behavior?

5. Will automated vehicles impact your employees?

6. How are you preparing to utilize new energy sources if it is regulated or demanded?

7. Will you be impacted by net neutrality?

8. How will you build in oversight of the artificial intelligence you used?

9. Are you prepared for increased oversight and regulation of data and privacy?

10. How do you protect the privacy of your employees on work devices?

11. How do you analyze the impact of future trends on your business? Do you do this at least annually?

12. What companies do you currently partner with?

    a. Do you consider the future trajectory of your partners?

13. If Google, Amazon, or Facebook are splintered in antitrust campaigns, will that impact your business?

14. Do you have a cohesive and holistic strategy around emerging technologies (i.e., do you have agreed assumptions about future trends)?

15. What timeline does your technology strategy address? How soon do you predict these trends will impact you?

16. How close are you to actively implement AI vs. your industry and competitors?

17. How will your company's human capital use artificial intelligence?

18. Who will you partner with to connect voice recognition, artificial intelligence, and things?

19. What are the potential consequences of how you use artificial intelligence?

20. How do you attract and retain talent through innovative programs?

Cybersecurity

Everything we do creates new vulnerabilities. How do you manage the unknown?

Cybersecurity threats are unlocked doors opened by vulnerability points left unchecked. As we add new technologies to our organizations, new vulnerabilities are created. As we change the way people work and live using technology, new vulnerability points are formed. As the infrastructure to daily life is more reliant on Internet connections, data clouds, and wireless nodes, the ability for hackers to target central services like transportation, financial services, and health care to wreak havoc or destabilize a region continues to increase.

Most directors do not have a technology background. That's okay. In fact, it may be a good thing so long as you are informed enough to ask the right questions and strong enough to hold your security team accountable.

This chapter will detail things to think about in cybersecurity, examples of what has gone wrong, and samples of companies that get these things right with best practices and approaches. It will give you a framework to manage the unknown.

The unfortunate reality is that an "Enron" moment in cybersecurity is likely on the horizon. When Christopher Wray, Director of the FBI, spoke to thousands of directors at the National Association of Corporate Directors Global Summit in 2018, he cited concerns that the virus or the malware that could be devastating to your company may already be in place; it has just not been activated. He reiterated it is not a matter *if*, but *when*, virtually every

© Jennifer C. Wolfe 2020
J. C. Wolfe, *Disruption in the Boardroom*, https://doi.org/10.1007/978-1-4842-6159-0_4

company, large and small, will be the victim of a data or cyber breach. In March of 2020, the FBI reported that financial losses due to cyberattacks in 2019 exceeded $3.5 billion and that the United States was not prepared to fend off cyberattacks. In the aftermath of the 2020 Coronavirus Pandemic and the massive remote work plans implemented, the threats of attack and crisis plans needed became more acute. In this chapter, I cover case studies to serve as prompts for table topics of discussion, questions to ask in your board meetings of fellow board members and the experts who serve in your company's leadership, as well as tools to help you assess your cyber risk readiness.

Case Studies: What Could Go Wrong?

Each year, data breaches make headlines and strike fear in senior executives and boards. Directors can learn from the mistakes of other organizations by understanding the source of the breach and asking their security teams as well as fellow board members how they would have handled the same breach. Case studies are important table topics for board lunch and dinner conversations. At your next board meeting, ask your fellow board members how you would handle the same issue and ask your senior executives how exposed you are to the same issue.

- **Capital One**. In July 2019, Capital One announced a massive data breach with more than 100 million Americans and six million Canadians impacted. The hacker responsible was a former software engineer for Amazon Web Services (AWS) who gained access by exploiting a misconfigured web application firewall. The company replaced its security chief four months after the disclosure. Experts opined that a common reason for this type of breach is how the company is managing its servers and where sensitive information is stored. Boosting the security of servers can reduce exposure to data breaches. Some claimed that Amazon's AWS servers were partially responsible, though Amazon denies this. Senators Ron Wyden and Elizabeth Warren both demanded the Federal Trade Commission investigate Amazon in the aftermath. Would you fire your security chief in the aftermath of a serious breach that caused harm to your customers?

- If you used a supplier like AWS, would you take action against them? Would the contracts you have with them allow that (hint, probably not)?

First American Financial. In 2019 hundreds of millions of documents related to mortgage deals going back to 2003 were compromised and made visible on its own website. The documents were inadvertently exposed on their own site without requiring login credentials. First American learned of a design defect in an application that made that type of unauthorized access possible. Other companies who have suffered from a similar glitch include Signet Jewelers, Panera Bread, and LifeLock. It's a good reminder that sometimes it's not even the result of a hacker, but a glitch in your own systems.

- How do you have checks and balances for your own systems to look for latent defects such as this?

- Do you have security teams test your own systems? Do you try to "hack" yourself?

State Farm. In August 2019, State Farm notified customers with the following: "State Farm recently detected an information security incident in which a bad actor used a list of user IDs and passwords obtained from some other source, like the dark web, to attempt to access State Farm online accounts. During our investigation, we determined that the bad actor possessed the user ID and password for your State Farm online account." This type of cyberattack is known as credential stuffing. Attackers buy or steal usernames and passwords that were leaked from other companies' data breaches and then try to log in to other accounts to gain access to information, largely motivated by financial reasons. Retailers are usually the top targets for this type of attack, but any company that has a login could be impacted by the same approach. Experts advise companies to require multiple forms of authentication that take location, physical device, and user identity into considerations. While the impact seemed minimal, the trust customers have in a brand is always at issue when there is a breach.

- How do you think your customers would react to this type of breach? How would you restore trust?

- How would you notify your customers?

Quest Diagnostics. Approximately 12 million patients had medical information and social security numbers compromised when there was an intrusion in 2019. Small in comparison to the 78 million impacted by the Anthem hack of 2015 (which was the result of two Chinese nationals), experts say that medical information is not really valuable to hackers, but financial information is. The breach was through a third-party vendor, American Medical Collection Agency, which is a billing collections vendor. Quest was able to discover the breach internally. Quest disclosed it with its SEC filings; however, the fallout came from the fact that the Quest customers were impacted by the failure of a third-party vendor – a company they didn't choose to have their medical billing records. With the information obtained, bad actors could open credit cards, take out loans, or intercept tax refunds of Quest customers. Consumers have a right to be upset. It raises a red flag about controls in place with key vendors. Target's breach in 2013 was also the result of an HVAC vendor. It's important that you are not only checking your own systems but monitoring vendors who have access to your systems or private information.

- Was the first public announcement of this in an SEC filing the right way to go?

- Would you do the same when faced with this information?

- How do you monitor vendors who have access to your systems or data?

DoorDash. DoorDash posted to its company blog that nearly five million customers, delivery workers, and merchants had their information stolen by hackers. The breach occurred on May 4, 2019, but it took the company almost five months to detect the breach. They, too, were impacted by a third-party service provider and that the last four digits of their credit cards or bank accounts were stolen. Delivery workers also had their driver's license information taken.

- Barring any legislation that requires faster notice, what do you think is a reasonable time to notify customers of a breach?

- Is it important to offer some restitution (i.e., a free LifeLock memberships or something that helps with identity theft?)

- What's the best way to notify your customers?

Facebook. Of course, one of the big recent breach stories was how Cambridge Analytica was able to access information from Facebook that it could use to target ads in the 2016 election. Facebook claims they didn't know. Cambridge Analytica used a third-party app developed by a researcher at Cambridge University's Psychometrics Center. Three hundred thousand people downloaded the app, which gave access to their friends' information on Facebook. Cambridge Analytica took this data and used it for political ads for the Trump campaign. This meant they obtained information on 87 million Facebook users without their direct consent. Facebook bore the brunt of this for not knowing how third-party apps were using data collected from its own site. It is a red flag to understand your company's use of social media and third-party apps. This raises an important question for directors to understand how their digital functions integrate with third-party apps and cross over into security protections. If your digital marketing group is not interfacing with security, how would this be discovered? Ask questions of your digital team to understand how Facebook data is used and how third-party apps integrate with your digital marketing. This incident was the awakening by Congress and the public at large that their social media data is a treasure trove for more than just Facebook. This exposure also prompted Facebook's new mantra that "the future is private" and that it will work to re-earn trust. The future is about privacy and the world's reaction to this story helps support that new narrative. As a director, think about your own privacy, as well as ask questions about your company's privacy strategy.

- How would you react to finding that a third party allowed access to your customer data?

- Would this have been viewed differently if the third party were trying to sell a product or promote a new show vs. pushing a political message?

- How does your company use Facebook, social media, and third-party apps? How does data transfer between them and you?

The Big Hack. On October 4, 2018, Bloomberg released a bombshell story reporting that China had infiltrated high-profile technology companies like Apple, Amazon Web Services, and others. The article detailed that the motherboards manufactured in China and used in servers by these high-profile companies had a chip implanted by the Chinese government that could later be activated for nefarious purposes. All of the companies denied it and Bloomberg doubled down on the story. While it was handed out at security conferences as a new mission statement for diligence in purchasing critical components to your security infrastructure from other vendors, many believe it was not accurate. Regardless of whether or not it is true, it is certainly possible, if not plausible. The Equifax breach was later determined to be sourced to the Chinese military, as was the Anthem breach. If China is capable of infiltrating companies that house sensitive data and steal it and expose it to the dark Web, it raises some important questions for board members.

- Where do you source your servers and critical components of your network security?

- Is any of it produced in China, Russia, or places that could have a reason to infiltrate your systems as a state actor? These are worthwhile conversations.

- What if China or another state actor could flip a switch and start a cyberattack against your company? What would you do? What immediate action would you take?

NotPetya. In 2017, the malware NotPetya spread from the servers of an unassuming Ukrainian software firm to some of the largest businesses worldwide, paralyzing their operations. These companies faced billions in damages.

- Merck $870,000,000
- FedEx $400,000,000
- Maersk $300,000,000
- Mondelez $188,000,000
- Plus, many others with a total damage over ten billion dollars

Where do you outsource IT infrastructure and network support? When you outsource outside of the United States, how do you know you are not exposing your network infrastructure to companies that could be corrupt or influenced by a corrupt government? What is your plan if malware attacks your company systems? How will you, as a board, communicate if your systems are shut down?

Sixty percent of the breaches in 2019 involved unpatched vulnerabilities (think Equifax). How does your company manage patching of licensed software, vendors, and open source code? Trust is central to the future, so is privacy.

Key Cybersecurity Responsibilities

I've been in some retail boardrooms where board directors question if their customers really care about privacy or if they would really be upset about a data breach. One general counsel told me that they *outsourced* their credit card processing, so it wouldn't really be "their problem" if a breach occurred. Every company is different, and I couldn't universally say that every company would lose trust of customers if there is a breach, but it is definitely a conversation you should be having in your boardroom.

- Will you lose customer trust if they feel their privacy or data has been compromised? The board needs to have a clear viewpoint on this issue to determine how much money to invest in cybersecurity.

- How would you react to malware like NotPetya shutting down your systems company-wide in a matter of minutes?

- How fast could you react and get reestablished?

- How would you communicate with employees? Customers?

- If you outsource data management or network infrastructure, is contractual indemnification enough in the event of a breach?

- Are you outsourcing outside of the United States? If so, what happens in the event of another pandemic or breach?

Best practices require spending some money. It's up to you to determine the balance between cost and benefit. Those are the tough decisions directors need to make when approving the company budget, and part of the board's function is to ensure that enough money is allocated to cover the risk profile the board determines is appropriate. It's all cost-benefit analysis and having a clear appetite for the risk. My hope in this chapter is that you are making those decisions fully informed and forming a risk appetite as it relates to cybersecurity. Generally speaking, experts suggest at least 1% of global revenue should be allocated to cybersecurity.

According to Verizon's annual report of breaches from 2019, there are some interesting statistics on which to focus your attention as a board member. In 2019, here's the breakdown of cyber breaches:

- 69% were perpetrated by outsiders

- 34% involved internal actors

- 23% were nation state actors

- 71% were financially motivated

- 25% were motivated by espionage

- 32% involved phishing

- 56% took months or longer to discover

- 52% featured hacking

- 33% included social attacks

- 28% involved malware

If we assume that most board members do not have a technology background, how do you focus your attention in the boardroom? What questions should you be asking? This topic in the boardroom has been around for a few years now. When you put it in the context of all of the new issues boards are facing, it's not surprising that boards are getting fatigued with the topic. According to an annual survey by the National Association of Corporate Directors, funding other initiatives more directly tied to growth may supersede cybersecurity. While cybersecurity has been the hot topic for many years, directors don't feel they need to spend any more time addressing it. Accordingly, we want to break down the most important areas for directors to address to prioritize time on the board agenda.

The key cybersecurity responsibilities for board members:

1. Identify your exposure points.

2. Know why someone might attack you.

3. Understand why breaches occur.

4. Learn what questions to ask.

In this process, you will develop an annual risk appetite and cost-benefit analysis to cybersecurity.

Identify Your Cybersecurity Exposure Points

Your first responsibility to oversee cybersecurity is to analyze your exposure to cybersecurity threats. The most common points of exposure are

- IT systems and network infrastructure
- IoT – physical and digital points of entry and security
- Data – cloud
- People

Your IT infrastructure (i.e., how your company's computers are all connected to the Internet and to each other), points of physical and digital entry and security and devices, and how you store your data are each exposure points that could be compromised by a weakness exposed, an unpatched vulnerability, a direct attack, or other means. The case studies presented each address some of these issues as examples. To fully provide oversight of these areas, you will need expertise to help you ask questions and ensure that you track, measure, and verify there are mitigation measures in place, as well as conduct a third-party independent audit of your systems. These areas get technical quickly and could be an entire book. There are courses for this level of technical detail in the context of the boardroom (check out NACD's Cybersecurity Oversight Program [nacdonline.org/events]). I also include questions at the end of the chapter that deal with these areas. An audit of exposure points is a useful tool and should be conducted at least every other year. For reference, boards annually hire outside auditors to audit financial records because they are required to do so. Boards also hire compensation experts to make recommendations on how they incent and compensate senior leadership. Why would boards not hire an outside auditor to evaluate their cybersecurity vulnerabilities?

Another important component to all cybersecurity exposure points is people. Talk to cybersecurity experts and they will usually tell you a "person" fails in some way and that allows the breach to occur. Boards should focus considerable attention in evaluating the "people" exposure point because when a person fails, that's when a board is likely to be held accountable and CEOs are often asked to resign. There are three big people areas to consider when it comes to the "people" problem:

1. Phishing
2. Inside jobs
3. Trust but verify information provided internally

Phishing

Verizon reported that 32% of data breaches in 2019 involved phishing. One of the biggest dangers of phishing is that the attackers are getting more and more sophisticated. Emails that look like they are from FedEx about a delivery or Microsoft about your email account or from someone you know often trick even the most tech savvy into clicking a dangerous link. I was once working with a client and a general counsel who was particularly focused on training related to phishing. Unfortunately, she was the one to inadvertently click a phishing link herself. Sometimes the intent of the phishing email is to scare you into immediate action, sometimes it is to entice you with money, and others appear to be from an organization you trust. Usually a close look will find typos or clues that something is not right.

Even people at the top of the organization can fall prey. In the 2016 presidential election, John Podesta, the head of Hillary Clinton's campaign, inadvertently clicked a phishing link. His story is important for a couple of reasons. First, he was using a Gmail account instead of a hillaryclinton.com account. I bring this up with boards because some boards allow their directors to use personal emails instead of a board-issued email. A good practice is for a company to provide directors a device to use exclusively for board activity and a secure email that is being monitored and tracked by the company security team. In Podesta's case, he was using a Gmail account and received a phishing email that his account had been hacked and he needed to reset his password. He forwarded it to campaign staffers, and they instructed him to reset the password with a secure link to Google and instructions to set up two-factor authentication. Unfortunately, a busy Podesta had not deleted the phish email and mistakenly went back to the original email, clicking a phishing link, opening the door to a hack that ultimately had negative ramifications to the Clinton campaign.

Phishing is not going away. Many email systems try to stop phishing before it gets through, but if it gets passed your systems, you need to be aware. Look out for red flags and signals to watch for:

- If the email comes in overnight: Many phishing emails come in during early morning hours.

- Typos: If you see a lot of typos in an email prompting you to click a link, be cautious and don't click those links; go directly to those providers.

- The language isn't quite right: It was written in another language and poorly translated to English.

- If an email is a prompt to reset a password and you didn't request that prompt, it is likely a phishing email.

- Email address isn't quite right: Looks different than it should (i.e., it is a .gov and it should be a .com or some other variation).

- Threatening you with something or intimidation tactics.

- Offering you something: A free iPhone or year's subscription if you fill out a survey.

- Bottom line, if you aren't sure, don't click it and send it to your security team.

- Be careful with your personal devices as well. As directors, you could be a target for spear phishing (i.e., you are the target). If your email is readily available in social media or you use it for purchasing items, it can be obtained and used to trick you.

- Also, watch for emails from friends with links. Sometimes bad actors can access your contact list and try to trick you with someone you think you know. Watch for all of these red flags.

Inside Jobs

Inside jobs are also a greater concern. Infamous whistleblower, Edward Snowden, wrote a book *Permanent Record*, to tell his side of his 2013 story of stealing National Security Agency intelligence to let the world know what the US government was doing with surveillance. In his book, he warns of the dangers coming with artificial intelligence and facial recognition. These are all points that are under greater scrutiny as we look at the unintended consequences of technology.

But his story is important for another security reason: insider jobs. How do you know if you have someone amid you who discovers something about your company, doesn't like it, and then wants to do you harm? Snowden, after all, was a contractor hired by Booz Allen Hamilton. He did not have a college degree. He was posting in online chat groups about how easy it was to get a job at the NSA and was disgruntled with things he was learning. No one caught this. Could you have young workers amid you that don't like something about your company? For example, what if someone doesn't like how you treat certain employees, the pay discrepancy between the top and the bottom, political ties you may have, or how you manufacture your goods, or any number of other reasons. Are you asking the right questions about who is being hired to work in your company, even short-term contractors who have access to your systems? Is your company really vetting not just employees but consultants and contractors? What about IT support workers offshored and under management separate from your company?

As one other example, Uber hired an ex-felon to serve as a "safety driver" of one of its test self-driving cars in Arizona. The driver was preoccupied with texting or something on the phone when the car hit and killed a biker. This wasn't malicious, but was it an oversight to allow an ex-felon to be a safety driver? For example, some states have begun to prohibit those with felony convictions from working for rideshare companies. How would you react on your board toward the chief human resources officer in the next board meeting? Would you say that wasn't his or her responsibility because it was so many layers deep in the organization? How would you hold the company leadership accountable?

How do you monitor for disgruntled employees? How do you ensure you have the right people in jobs that if they fail, could erode trust in your judgment? Human Resources (HR) should be using tools to help monitor online activity of network infrastructure workers or those with access to sensitive information. Certainly, activity at work, but also there are new social monitoring and artificial intelligence–driven software tools to monitor people of concern.

Trust but Verify and then Listen to the People You Hire

Finally, on the people front, the most vital function you perform as a director is to trust but verify the information provided to you from your security and information technology team, your legal team, and your Human Resources team. Your security and information technology team are responsible for the core exposure points systems and network infrastructure, servers, patching and technology, points of vulnerability, and your data and cloud infrastructure. Your legal team should be checking for compliance with the policies put in place. And your HR team is responsible for vetting all employees and looking for potential disgruntled employees or vendors who access technology. Your entire c-suite needs to be working, together, and not in silos, to ensure the security of your company. Your role is oversight. Are those leaders incented to work together or are their goals potentially misaligned as to eliminate the incentive for them to check one another and work together? Are their incentives such that they won't likely report small breaches to you because it impacts their bonus? Does this mean you have created an environment where you won't ever have a full picture of what's actually going wrong until it's too late?

One final point on this, if you do hire good people to advise you on cybersecurity, you need to listen to them. In 2018 security executives from Facebook, Google, and Twitter all left amid failure for the board and senior executives to listen to them. At Facebook, Alex Stamos had continued to express concerns about Russian interference on Facebook's platform during the 2016 election and did not feel senior executives were listening to him. After his resignation, senior leadership disassembled the team and spread out security across engineering functions.

You may not like what you are hearing. It might cost too much money to do what they advise. But it sure doesn't look good publicly if they leave and then something happens. You need to listen and then determine the cost-benefit analysis of correcting the problems identified and whether or not it aligns with your overall company strategy and brand value.

Why Might Someone Attack You?

The second responsibility as a director is to have a candid conversation with your fellow directors about why your company might be targeted. The primary reason is typically to access data that can be used for financial gain, but there are other reasons. Do you possess information that can be used to steal someone's identity or access a credit card or financial account? Or are you in an industry where shutting you down could wreak havoc. For example, energy, medical or hospitals, transportation, banking, or telecommunications. These are the fairly obvious ones. If you are in one of those industries, you likely have a top-of-the-line approach to security with hefty budgets to support the risk.

But there are other issues that require focus and attention. Disgruntled employees or angry groups are also of increasing concern. Do you treat your suppliers fairly and pay them timely? If you repeatedly leave suppliers or vendors exposed, they could become disgruntled and target you. Who might be unhappy with decisions you make? Have honest conversations about these issues to pinpoint exposure areas.

Espionage by a competitor is also a rarer occurrence, but always a possibility. Consider who might have a desire to cause you harm. How could they infiltrate your organization? Finally, there is also the potential for stock manipulation and outright blackmail of your senior executives. In the aftermath of the Me Too Movement, this has become increasingly an issue, particularly of personal devices. If your senior executives have engaged in "bad behavior" and there is a digital record of it, expect that someone may try to "hack" in and get that proof to make their point.

The following are a few examples of why you might be targeted:

- Financial information
- Blackmail – embarrassing information
- Stock manipulation
- Societal disruption – state actor
- Health-care information
- Competitor – theft of intellectual property or invalidation of key intellectual property
- Disgruntled employee, contractor, vendor

Why Breaches Occur and When to Get Outside Perspective

Your third responsibility as a director is to understand why breaches occur and when you need outside help – this is what oversight is all about. Depending upon the size of your organization, you likely have a cybersecurity team to ensure the security of your company. It's not realistic or practical to assume that a group of 6–10 directors could provide comprehensive oversight of such a rapidly changing highly technical area. This is why getting outside perspective is so critical and understanding why breaches occur is necessary to hold management accountable and ensure they have the right resources to deliver.

An emerging best practice is to periodically engage an outside firm to run a "health check" of your company's security initiatives. Some might call it an audit. Much like the modern-day practices of audit emerged after Sarbanes–Oxley (enacted in response to the Enron scandal), the same is likely coming in cybersecurity. Savvy boards are one step ahead. High-risk or targeted companies in areas of telecommunications, energy, and health care are already doing this regularly.

Additionally, many boards have formed a technology or security committee or subcommittee of audit. Those committees can hire outside, objective advisors to assist them in analyzing information presented, giving alternative points of view and serving as a "gut check" for what information is provided. According to the 2019–2020 National Association of Corporate Directors Public Company Governance Survey, only 2% of new board seats were filled with directors experienced in cybersecurity. With boards more focused on volatility and future business models, boards are citing a need for better oversight structures vs. more time on the subject. The board is not yet legally required to have someone with cyber experience, but if you do not, it is a good practice to have an objective, independent advisor who works exclusively with the board (i.e., don't hire the person who makes millions working with your Chief Information Security Officer (CISO) – they are biased; inherently, hire someone independent who only works for the board).

If something does occur, even if it seems small, it is important to understand the root cause. If you don't know the root cause, it will happen again. To discover the root cause, it's helpful to use a technique often referred to as the 5 Whys. Basically, ask yourself "why" five times and your fifth answer will give you the root cause.

Let's use the example of a breach due to failure to patch open source code:

1. Why did the breach happen?

    a. Bad actors discovered that we had not patched open source code and used that to enter our system.

2. Why did that happen?

    a. We had not patched the open source code and they tested our systems to find the vulnerability.

3. Why did that happen?

    a. We didn't timely realize that we had not patched the open source code, so they exploited it.

4. Why did that happen?

    a. We don't have a policy or procedure for patching open source code so no one was paying attention to it.

5. And why did that happen?

    a. The leadership who oversees this did not make this a priority because they were focused on other issues.

    b. There was no budget for people or software resources to address this.

So, who is accountable in this scenario?

- General Counsel should be overseeing policies and procedures to protect the company and serve as a check and balance in open source code; that didn't happen.

- Chief security officer should put in place a policy and procedure to patch open source code and that didn't happen.

- Information technology should serve as a cross-check to ensure that all open source code is tracked, and patches are tracked and that didn't happen.

- Budgets should be allocated for the work necessary to do this and that didn't happen.

Learn What Questions to Ask

Finally, your most important role as a director in cybersecurity is to continually learn what questions to ask and what top trends to be following as best practices. I've included here a few of the emerging trends in cybersecurity and questions to ask.

- **Privacy compliance**

  - How will our customers react if we compromise their "private" information?

  - What is that worth in cybersecurity spending?

  - What laws will impact us in the future and how are we preparing to comply?

  - Are we taking the highest standards and working toward that or working toward a lower standard, and if so, why?

- **Open source compliance**

  - How do we patch open source code? For that matter, how are you patching all code?

  - Are devices timely updated?

  - What tools do we use?

  - What outside help do we use?

  - What about vendors?

- **Readiness for artificial intelligence (AI)**
  - How are we using AI?
  - What unintended consequences could occur?
  - What is our viewpoint on the corporate responsibility for bias in AI?

- **Ransomware preparedness**
  - What happens if we are hit with a ransomware attack?
  - What is our viewpoint on paying out money to regain access to our systems?
  - Do we need to have Bitcoin or some cryptocurrency on hand if it is needed?
  - Is there a threshold where we pay to get our business back on track or keep it out of the press?
  - Does that create a slippery slope and make us a future target?
  - How do we interact with law enforcement?

- **Malware, phishing, inside jobs**
  - What is our plan if we are hit with malware? What steps are taken to slow and stop the spread?
  - Where do we buy our IT support? Network infrastructure components? Are we at risk if a state actor can take control of our systems?
  - How do we ensure that the people working for us are not disgruntled?
  - How do we continually train about phishing and monitor to stop phishing?
  - How do we as a board watch for spear phishing on our personal devices?

- **Crisis communication preparedness**
  - What is our plan if something catastrophic occurs?
  - How do we convene and what is our approach? Apologies may not be sufficient; what responsibility do we have to customers, employees?
  - What will we provide to the media?

- **Internet of things (IoT) lockdown**
  - If something happens and our systems are compromised, how do we quickly lock down all devices and vulnerability points?
  - What if that doesn't happen, how do we get back online?
  - How do we communicate this to the public?
- **Personal devices**
  - Should board members be issued personal devices and emails used only for board purposes?
  - How do you ensure your personal device is not the target of spear phishing?
- **Audit, check, and check again – trust but verify**
  - How do we trust but verify what we are being told?
  - Should we be getting a third-party audit of our security initiatives?
  - Should we have a technical advisory panel for the board to regularly assist us on cybersecurity initiatives?

I've included more questions at the end of the chapter. This is a continuous exercise. You are never done and can never check the box as though this one is completed. Cybersecurity vulnerabilities, mitigation tactics, and solutions are in a continual state of flux. This is why continuous learning and discipline in the boardroom is so difficult and yet paramount at the same time.

Legislation Is Coming – What May You Be Required to Do in the Future

Legislation in the United States is already pending in areas of cybersecurity. It is one of those areas that is fairly bipartisan. So, at some point, expect this type of legislation to be enacted. And, if there is an Enron moment, it will be fast tracked and much more onerous. These are just a few of the laws pending that could impact your organization:

- Federal Autonomous Vehicle Legislation – SELF Drive Act
    - This bill has had stops and starts for several years (no pun intended). The intention is to provide a federal framework for safety to support self-driving technology and its development, testing, and deployment. It was initially passed in the House in 2017, but then failed in the Senate. It is back in the House and will likely, eventually, be taken up and reconsidered. It's important because more than half of the states have enacted some of their own legislation. Like many areas of cybersecurity and data privacy, this fragmented approach makes it difficult for organizations to plan for and manage compliance.

- Cybersecurity Disclosure Act of 2017
    - Introduced in 2017 and then again in 2019, the intention is to amend the Securities and Exchange Act to promote transparency in the oversight of cybersecurity risks at publicly traded companies. It would require companies to disclose whether or not any member of the board is a cybersecurity expert, and if not, why having this expertise on the board is not necessary because of other steps taken by the company.

- State Legislatures pending bills related to cybersecurity
    - According to Jones Day law firm, California has a law that took effect on January 1, 2020, to mandate that manufacturers that sell or offer to sell a connected device in California equip the device with reasonable security features. This law can only be enforced by the attorney general or by the state or local government, and it is unclear exactly how it will be enforced.

    - According to the National Conference of State Legislatures, 43 states introduced bills or resolutions that deal with cybersecurity in 2019.[1] These include key areas:

---

[1] A detailed list by state can be found here: www.ncsl.org/research/telecommunications-and-information-technology/cybersecurity-legislation-2019.aspx

- Creating a task force or commission to oversee cybersecurity

- Restructure government for improved security

- Study use of blockchain for cybersecurity

- Provide security of utilities and critical infrastructure

- Exempt cybersecurity operations from public records laws

- Address security of connected devices

- Regulate cybersecurity within the insurance industry

- Provide funding for improved security measures

- Address cybersecurity threats to elections

- SEC Cyber Unit

  - The SEC is evaluating its role to regulate cybersecurity issues with creation of a Cyber Unit in 2017. It enforced the first action against a company in 2018.

- General Data Protection Regulation (GDPR)

  - Europe's stringent law applies to all businesses that collect and process personal data of European residents. It took effect on May 25, 2018. As of this writing, are still watching to see how the EU will enforce this law and what penalties may be enforced. A few key points:

    - The primary purpose of the law was to provide citizens the right to control their data. For example:

      - Right to be informed (must provide specific consent for data to be used or tracked – a very specific opt in).

      - Children are protected to a greater extent (they cannot consent).

      - Right to be forgotten.

      - Right to object to how they are portrayed.

- Gives citizens the right to be notified of a breach within 72 hours.

    - Penalty for failure to comply up to 4% of revenue.

- California has a similar law which goes into effect in 2020 and is "GDPR light." Other states will likely follow, or we will see national legislation to protect privacy rights of customers.

Additionally on the subject of privacy, in January of 2020, Amazon engineers went to the media with alarming concerns that devices like Ring need to be shut down amid privacy concerns. Digital predators often target young people. In one instance with a Ring camera, a hacker tormented a young girl in her playroom, seemingly for fun. In more dangerous scenarios, bad actors entice young girls into performing sexual acts on camera and then blackmail them to continue to perform those acts. Cameras are very dangerous in an interconnected world that can so easily be hacked. Combined with the damaging impact of social media to our younger generations, this type of criminal activity will also see increased legislation and activity. If your company relies upon usage of cameras or microphones, be on the lookout for legislation that may require you to change how you operate or require more stringent opt-in settings for consumers. Look for opportunities to provide greater safety for children and teenagers, in particular. Also, if you have young people in your life, help them understand that cameras should be covered or turned off when not in use and only used with people you know and trust.

Despite all of these concerns, after the 2020 Coronavirus Pandemic, many health experts cite tracking individuals, and their points of contact could be essential to stopping the spread of a pandemic in the future. What will happen to our privacy expectations when the "public good" demands to know where we have been? Expect to see more legislation at a state and federal level related to privacy. For boards, understanding the changing dynamics in what is legally required is important. While your general counsel and security team are likely considering these issues carefully and developing important outside resources, the important question is do you wait until it's required or start the process now. As a board, have a clear point of view around this issue. Privacy directly intersects with cybersecurity. While they each deserve their own attention, legislation related to cybersecurity will be directly impacted by privacy policy concerns.

Who Is Getting This Right?

The problem we have in cybersecurity is no security executive wants to run around touting how great their security is for fear that that makes them a target. It does. Accordingly, we don't see a lot of media stories or use cases out there of companies getting it right. We see a lot of what goes wrong, but not a lot of what goes right. Most of the best practices we get come from the security providers and consulting companies. They are consolidating the good and the bad into best practices without pointing out any one specific company. I don't recommend any company brag about their security; it absolutely makes you a target.

One of the recent breaches discussed in Chapter 4, Capital One, was recognized by experts as "getting it right": Given that the average time for a breach to be discovered hovers around 2971 days, the short timeline associated with the incident shows that Capital One knows the measures it must take when a breach does occur. The arrest was made a mere 12 days after the initial vulnerability report, which is light speed in the industry, commented the chief technology officer for cyber protection solutions at Raytheon.

A few best practices at the board level cited by experts:

- Have a chief information security officer.

- Spend at least 1% of global revenue on cybersecurity.

- Design in security when developing new programs, technologies, and so on.

- Utilize models for valuing your risk factors. There are many different ones out there; pick one or two and benchmark yourself regularly. Ask management to follow these same principles so you can build your expertise in evaluating the information presented.

- Document cybersecurity policies and practices.

- Continually educate yourself on changes in cyber practices.

- Understand trends provided by the Information Sharing and Analysis Center related to your industry; this can help you compare how you are doing with others.

- Develop a risk profile so you can make right decisions in balancing risks with investment. There's no magic bullet or right solution, it's all about balancing. This means you have a clear and agreed-upon risk profile and understanding of your exposure.

- Ask tough questions related to passwords and human or people errors (i.e., phishing, passwords, lax access to secure areas).

- Ask the questions cited throughout this chapter on a regular basis.

The Factor Analysis of Information Risk (FAIR) Institute also provides good benchmarking assessments. BitSight also provides standards in security ratings. Firms like CrowdStrike also provide benchmarking. Of course, all the big accounting and consulting firms also specialize in these areas using several generally accepted risk assessment methods. There is no shortage of places to go to get an outside perspective on cyber risk management. What follows is a framework that you can use to evaluate your oversight of cyber-risk.

Cybersecurity Framework for Discussion and Decision Making in the Boardroom

Outlined as follows are basic questions and issues you should be addressing with your fellow directors and with your chief information security officer, general counsel, and chief human resources officer. To use this scoring mechanism, plan a discussion with your senior leadership team. Ask them the questions posed in the following text. After hearing their answers, give each category a score of 1–5 based upon the prompts as follows.

1	2	3	4	5
Not even on the radar	**Aware, but do not address**	**Some activity but not a priority**	**Priority in progress**	**Fully address**

- **People *Score:* _____**
  - Phishing
    - Do you regularly and objectively check for phishing? How do you hold everyone (from the top to the bottom) equally accountable if they click a phishing link?
  - Use of personal devices and emails
    - Do you diligently track use of company vs. personal devices and require employees and board members to use company emails that can be tracked and shut down if necessary?
    - Do you block employees from accessing websites, clicking links, or accessing cloud servers that could be harmful? How do you monitor and know?

- Social media monitoring
  - Do you track senior executives on social media?
  - Do you use software to identify if employees are negatively impacted by company policies or if an employee is becoming disgruntled?
  - Do you use software to track emails for the same?
- Employment agreements
  - Do your employment agreements clearly stipulate the requirements of employees to maintain confidential information and assign over their work product?
  - Do your employment agreements provide for privacy expectations?
- Is an incident response plan in place for employees who violate policies?
- Do you use some type of software to track employees with access to sensitive information or network security to check for insider jobs? What about your vendors?

- **Systems and Connection Points** *Score:* _____
  - How are your systems and connection points monitored for intrusion?
  - Do you threat test the system regularly?
  - Do you use outside testers to ensure integrity of the system?
  - Do you have your physical security measured tested regularly?

- **Malware and Network Security** *Score:* _____
  - Have you caught malware entering the system previously?
  - How did you address it?
  - Did you use the 5 Why methodology to get at the root cause?
  - Do you have a sufficient budget for addressing malware and network security?
  - How do you allow different c-suite executives to provide checks and balances to each other?

- **Cloud and Data** *Score:* _____
  - Which vendors do you use for cloud? How do you know they are safe? What is their risk mitigation plan? If they fail, what happens?
  - How do you prevent information stored in your cloud from being stolen?
  - What is your recourse if data is compromised?
  - What alternatives do you have?
  - What is your response plan?
- **Vendor Management** *Score:* _____
  - Do you actively monitor all vendors who have access to your systems or your physical offices?
  - Do you evaluate the security of vendors?
  - At what threshold (i.e., cost or access) do you monitor vendor access?
  - Do you timely pay vendors, particularly technology vendors?
  - Do you outsource services or devices and components to countries that could be a state actor (i.e., China, Ukraine, Russia, etc.)?
- **Open Source and Software Patching** *Score:* _____
  - Do you have a software patching policy?
  - Do you have an open source code policy for patching?
  - Do you have an open source code contribution policy for employees?
  - Do you use software to monitor patches?
  - How do you check that your policies and procedures are enforced?
- **Crisis Readiness** *Score:* _____
  - What is your communication plan if a cyber breach occurs?
  - What if your systems go down, how will you react?
  - Have you conducted a table talk exercise on how you respond?

- Will you use social media to respond to a crisis?

- Will you talk to traditional media? If so, when, and what will you say?

- How will you develop a mitigation plan?

- **Business Continuity** *Score:* _____

    - What is your plan for continuity if your systems are shut down?

    - What if a health, environmental, or disaster strikes? What is your plan for business continuity of your systems and integrity of your network?

    - Is this system tested regularly?

    - If you need to work remotely, are you prepared from a cyber standpoint to do this safely?

    - Does your workforce have work devices that can be monitored remotely?

- **Policies and Oversight** *Score:* _____

    - Are all of your cybersecurity measures documented?

    - Which group serves as an auditor to confirm compliance with policies you set?

    - How do you measure success?

    - Does your program include elements from recognized security standards such as ISO and NIST?

- **Protection of Intellectual Property** *Score:* _____

    - How do you protect the data and secrets of intellectual property within your systems?

    - Do you separate the "critical" intellectual property from other intellectual property?

    - How do you ensure that intellectual property is not internally taken?

- **Privacy** *Score:* _____

    - What is your compliance plan with GDPR?

    - What is your compliance plan in the United States under changing state by state guidelines?

    - What is your policy for protecting the privacy of employees?

- How do you ensure compliance with your privacy plan?
- How do you protect the privacy of your customers?
- **Oversight of Artificial Intelligence Score: _____**
  - How do you use artificial intelligence in the company?
  - How do you ensure there are not biases or unintended consequences?
  - What do you do to oversee this function?
- **Exposure Points Score: _____**
  - What are your core exposure points?
  - What is the mitigation strategy for each exposure point?
  - Physical premises. How do you use mitigation methods: camera, alarms, computer hardware, software, or firmware?
  - Who could sue you if there is a breach?
    - Customers?
    - Individuals?
    - Employees?
    - Financial institutions?
    - Shareholders?
- **Budget and Investment Score: _____**
  - Have you assessed your risk profile? What is your likelihood of an event occurring and what is the cost to you if it occurs? What is the value of mitigating against that risk?
  - Do you have enough budget allocated to the risk profile of your company?
  - How does the cost investment align with the value proposition to your stakeholders?
  - How do you prioritize based upon highest exposure to risk and highest impact?

- **Cyber Risk Insurance** *Score:* _____

  - How do you work with your insurance provider to evaluate your exposure? What about other vendors?

  - What will your insurance cover and what won't it cover?

  - Run exercises to evaluate potential scenarios and what insurance would cover and what it will not.

  - Keep in mind your insurance partners are there to help you, but also to sell insurance.

  - Has legal counsel provided you a matrix of all laws to which you are responsible for protecting information? For example, health care, financial, personal information, and so on. Ask legal counsel to give your specific company an audit of all laws under which you are accountable and an annual health check of how you are doing.

  - Are you sufficiently disclosing your cyber risks in your SEC filings?

- **Cross-Functional Checks and Balances** *Score:*

  _____

  - Do your General Counsel, CISO, head of information technology, marketing, and Human Resources meet at least quarterly to discuss how they work together to address cyber vulnerabilities across the organization?

  - Do executives other than your CISCO or head of IT have a voice and ability to speak to the board about cyber and security threats?

  - Do your executives allow for robust discussion on how to make improvements on a regular basis?

  - Are nontechnical leaders permitted culturally to raise questions about the latest technologies? Do you allow for cross-functional checks and balances?

How did your score? Did you have more 1s and 2s or 4s and 5s? Where you have low scores, you now need to ask yourself if more money and resources is needed to bring up those scores or if it is adequate for the risk you face. There are four ways for you to address the risks you have identified: transfer the risk to third party, accept the risk as a cost of doing business, mitigate the risk with resources, or avoid the risk with significant investment. See Figure 4-1.

Figure 4-1. Risk Accountability

For each of the areas in the framework you scored a 1 or a 2, ask how you view the risk, do you accept it, mitigate it, avoid it, or transfer it to someone else? What will you do with those risks? Use the chart above and note how you have allocated accountability of those risks.

Another way to address each risk factor where you scored a 1 or a 2 is to consider the following. Where do you plot the risk within the matrix shown in Figure 4-2? In which quadrant do you place the risk?

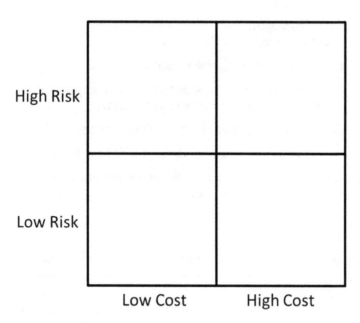

Figure 4-2. Risk Assessment

There are many tools to audit and evaluate your exposure points. I have included just a couple of them here. Whatever methodology you use, ensure you continuously update it and review it annually.

There are also a number of red flags to watch for:

- Management presentations focus on technology adoption instead of what problem it solves.

- More than half of the board members do not have a clear understanding of the impact of new disruptive technologies to business strategy.

- Lack of shared vision.

- Excessive use of acronyms or technical jargon to intimidate less technical board members.

- Majority of board presentations focus on preservation of past assets or value instead of future problems-solving and value.

- Management is too reluctant to change when needed.

- Learnings and education focus on hype vs. practical applications and challenges.

- Board's reaction is reactive vs. proactive.

- Risk dashboards used focus too much on known risks and not enough on unknown risks.

- Lengthy presentations fail to address questions.

- The CEO does not allow subject matter experts inside the organization to present to the board.

- Senior leadership is not open to dissenting points of view.

- Misalignment of incentives throughout the organization.

- CEO focused too much on financials and not sufficiently enough on cyber risk culture.

Conclusion

The most important rule when it comes to oversight of cybersecurity is to know that you are never done. Whatever checklist you are working from or framework you are using, by the time you complete it, the checklist has changed and there are new questions to ask. As technology changes and people change, new vulnerabilities are constantly created.

No matter how things change, there will always be the basic framework for success in the boardroom:

- Asking the right questions

- Verifying information

- Monitoring an internal and external system of checks and balances

- Reevaluating risk appetite and cost-benefit analysis of investment in cyber programs

Discussion Questions for the Boardroom

Throughout this chapter, I've provided questions for you to be asking related to the topics. I won't repeat them here, but what follows are reframed discussion questions to have at your board dinner or luncheon. Also, don't forget to use the case studies at the beginning of the chapter as discussion starters.

- What creates the most fear for you?

- Where do you think your greatest exposure point is?

- How do you measure success in monitoring these issues?

- How do you trust but verify what you are told by management?

- How are you monitoring phishing?

- How are you updating and patching software on business and personal devices? What about open source code?

- Do you have written policies to govern these issues?

- How do you manage supply chain vulnerabilities?

- Do you audit your cybersecurity independently?

- How does your committee work to manage cyber threats?

- Have you done table exercises/crisis response planning?

- What is your risk profile for cybersecurity?

- How do you develop a cost-benefit analysis for cyber risks?

- On every breach, do you use the 5 Whys approach (ask why five times to understand the root cause of why the breach occurred)?

- Have you identified your most critical assets that you cannot afford to lose and/or systems for handling unplanned outages? What are your digital crown jewels?

- Who has access to your digital information, and how?

- How are all the access points and exposure points managed?

- How do vendors access data about your company? How do they store company data on their own systems?

- What cloud-based services do you use to store information?

- How are passwords assigned and changed regularly?

- Can flash drives be used? Which shared drives can employees access? How do you know they don't use their personal drives?

- What happens if you are blackmailed?

- What happens if you are attacked – how do you convene to make immediate decisions and minimize exposure?

- What insurance do you have in place? What can and can't it do?

- What zero-tolerance policy is needed in the organization for security breaches or lapses in security measures?

- Who would likely attack you, and why?

- Have you been informed on prior attacks and how severe they were?

- How will you know if we have been hacked or breached?

- How are security clearances provided to employees? What about guests? Are they checked periodically and benchmarked against performance reviews?

- Do you monitor social media or online posts of employees with critical access to information?

- Where do senior management, legal, marketing, and the IT team differ on how they handle digital information? (This could be one of the most important and yet difficult pieces of information to get for oversight.)

- Do your vendors have clear cybersecurity measures in place? Do you monitor those measures?

- How are you addressing the security vulnerabilities of a mobile workforce?

- What are you doing to protect privacy and personally identifiable information, and how are we as a board ensuring that the right policies are in place? When and how are we using encryption?

The Future of Work and Societal Shifts

Millennials and Gen Z are our future leaders amid a profound shift in how we all live and work. How will you cultivate a path for them to lead the organization of the future?

The sharing economy, Millennials, Gen Z, and robots in the workforce are all just a few of the headline-grabbing signals about the future of work and how society is changing. In this chapter, I'll explore some of the big trends to watch and offer suggestions to consider as you contemplate the future of your workforce from the boardroom. You can also consider these trends as it impacts your customer base.

Changes will come in how people work and how they integrate with robotics, automation, and "smart" everything. The changes in how people work and live their lives directly impact what they need as consumers and what businesses need to meet future demands. As part of your role in oversight of the corporation, it's important to have a clear understanding of how the workforce will change and how societal shifts will impact your business model.

© Jennifer C. Wolfe 2020
J. C. Wolfe, *Disruption in the Boardroom*, https://doi.org/10.1007/978-1-4842-6159-0_5

Most of today's board members are squarely in the Baby Boomer category, with a few from Gen X and a rare few from the Millennial category. Pew Research regularly provides updates on generational data. According to their 2019 reports, there are approximately 85 million Millennials and 80 million Gen Z in the United States. Boomers are numbered at about 77 million and Gen X, the smallest of the living generation, tops off at about 64 million. This means that the younger two generations far outnumber the older two in the workforce and as consumers, even as life span is increased. In the boardroom, directors must be looking ahead to how they will serve their future customers and how they will manage a changing workforce.

Gen Z	Born 1996 and Later
	85 Million
Millennials	Born 1979-1995
	85 Million
Gen X	Born 1965-1978
	65 Million
Baby Boomers	Born 1946-1964
	77 Million

Figure 5-1. Generations in the Workforce

While much of this is context for making other decisions, the board's role is increasingly important when it comes to company culture and long-term thinking about work trends. These future work trends can impact investment decisions in office space, capital improvements, technology, and human resources.

First, since Millennials and Gen Z make up a majority of the workforce and are set to become tomorrow's leaders, we'll take a look at how they impact the workforce.

Millennials

The Millennial approach to work and life has shaped the last ten years in a social media culture. Many studies have generalized how they view and approach work, which can be helpful in making assumptions for decision making. Like any generalization, not everyone fits the rule, but provides guidance in understanding the future of work. They don't live to work; they work to live and care much more about travel and experiences than accumulating things. They don't care much about the corner office and would much prefer to work in groups (whether in person or virtually), collaborate and feel like what they are doing is contributing to something bigger than themselves. Companies have responded by creating more shared workspaces and building more collaborative teams than decades ago. Additionally, important perks like flexibility with scheduling, the ability to work remotely, and providing food and fun at work have become hallmarks of companies needing to attract a large number of this younger generation. They have often been dubbed the *entitlement* generation brought about by "concierge" style of parenting that took care of everything for them and, at times, sheltered them from negative comments. Millennials have parents who are either Baby Boomers (many of whom waited until later to have children) and Gen Xers (who shifted toward getting married and having children at a younger age). Which group their parents fell into can often shape their approach to life.

This generation is also more demanding about what they need to consider when working somewhere and that has given them more power than prior generations in negotiating what they will or will not accept. They are less loyal, though some could argue, so are most corporations today. Millennials will move on to new opportunities and are constantly curating a version of themselves. They came of age around the time of the 2008 financial crisis. Despite the fact that the economy has grown year after year since then (up until the 2020 Coronavirus Pandemic), they have a dystopian belief that the economy is bad and can't be trusted. Social media shaped their self-opinion often with unattainable goals about health, wellness, appearance, and fun. But many are beginning to cut that social media cord as they move into the stage of life where they begin to have families and other priorities amid concerns about privacy in the wake of artificial intelligence, biometrics, and facial recognition. Millennials are emerging now as leaders in corporations, as well as in elected government positions. Unlike prior generations, they actually tell each other how much they make and give suggestions on how to negotiate for what they want – very much more of the "sharing" culture than prior generations. Expect to see changes in how they manage others and what they expect of companies to keep them, particularly if they are talented.

Expect to see Millennials demand more of corporations when it comes to environmental and social issues (see Chapter 6). Also expect them to demand more in the way of flexibility and the ability to work remotely. Many of them have been saddled with student debt and are just now achieving some sense of financial independence and path toward their future. Accordingly, they are flocking out of big cities to find more affordable living and will expect corporations to facilitate that move.

Generation Z

Generation Z was born after 1998 and into the early 2000s. They are now in high school, college, and just beginning to enter the workforce. This generation came of age with smart phones and access to the Internet as a part of daily life. They have been trained about dangers of social media and cyberbullying since kindergarten. Much of the research on this generation has identified that generally speaking, they are seeking a more authentic life than Millennials, they are not a Facebook generation. They are not loyal. They will flock to the next social media platform quickly and abandon old ones. They use social media primarily to stay connected with friends, though, like millennials are suffering a lack of one-one social interaction. They watch YouTube videos of other people doing fun things like play video games. They believe they could learn almost anything from online videos. They don't want anything that doesn't have value to them – this will change the way they are marketed to as consumers. They don't want to be saddled with college debt, and many are seeking less risky pathways forward. They have grown up with school shooting drills and are now numb to the tragedy of school shootings. They are fearful that the environment has been ruined and could be irreparable. In the aftermath of the 2020 Coronavirus Pandemic, they will approach life cautiously with social distancing becoming a potential new normal in the years ahead. It will impact how they plan for the life they want to have in the future. They also tend to be more of the rule follower than the Millennials. Much like Baby Boomers were the radicals, challenging societal rules in the 1960s, and Gen Xers then followed the rules put before them in the 1990s, Gen Z do not seem to be as disruptive of a force as the Millennials, but time will tell as they move into full adulthood in the 2020s. While they are less risky in tackling life experiences like driving, drinking alcohol, and dating, they are more optimistic about the concept of starting your own business or approaching work in a nontraditional approach.

Gen Z grew up in a time of mobility and multiple realities and social networks and are true digital natives. They like a sense of community; they are realistic and are not as self-identifying as Millennials. They will value uniqueness and ethics above luxury or status like their Gen Xer parents did. They will think in terms of subscriptions and "time" and want things that are unlimited. This generation will be more motivated by security but will prefer to work alone vs. in communal settings like the Millennials. After the 2020 Coronavirus Pandemic, they will think about work differently. They will be prepared to work remotely and in collaboration via technology. They will be better at multitasking because they grew up doing it with smart devices. Companies may have to adjust to this generation working much more like their Gen Xer parents than the Millennials in between. It will create issues for leaders in

Human Resources as Millennials become their bosses. Like the Millennials, they will expect the workforce to conform to their needs. They are also more financially prepared than their millennial counterparts. Many are skipping costly education and preparing for a career directly from high school. They didn't experience the 2008 crash and recession that followed so they have a different outlook and approach. The 2020 Coronavirus Pandemic and economic fallout will, however, impact their view on investing in college and instill a preparedness mindset. Most of them won't take on debt in the same way their millennial counterparts did, which could help them be more financially prepared for their future and, in many ways, better off financially in the decades ahead. It could lead to starting families at a younger age than the millennials did, much like Gen Xers.

Gen Z will be important to the future of the workforce because they may be the first generation to truly work side by side robots and will have to consider a career path that is different than the generations before them. They are also the first generation who will have no memory whatsoever of life before the Internet or smart phones.

As board directors, it is important to understand what motivates these generations and what will need to be built into the culture of the organization. A few key takeaways to consider in attracting and retaining talent from Millennials and Gen Z:

- Show the company cares about people, employees, customers, the environment – they want to feel connected to something more meaningful.

- Provide flexibility. They will be accountable if you show them how, but want flexibility to live their life, not get to the corner office.

- Make work fun, create the ability to interact, and collaborate.

- Help them understand the mission of the company and why their work is important to fulfilling it.

- Give Gen Z a secure path to the future.

- Be willing to adapt to Millennials' demands if they are accountable for their work.

- If you have not already, start developing a solid exit strategy for Baby Boomers. Gen Xers need a chance to lead and pass on what they can to your organization with millennials already on their heels.

- Tap into the leadership and structure of Gen Xers to help through this transition while giving them a successful exit in the next ten years.

- Invest in tools and technology to allow for more remote work with accountability.

- Look for opportunities to incorporate charitable giving, community participation, and a sense of doing something that makes a difference as part of their work experience.

- Identify talent and be willing to adjust the work schedule and methods to meet their needs.

- Invest in education and skill building to build upon raw talent and ability vs. expecting them to come to you with it. Provide more training and career building.

- Invest in mental health support services to help them through difficult times.

- Consider providing many of the "services" that they need at a reduced cost (i.e., hair and beauty care, health and wellness, dog care, childcare, grocery, concierge-style services, travel and vacation planning, etc.).

- Create opportunities for senior executives to engage with younger workers in a town hall–like setting that allows for questions and a sense of accountability while also creating community. Help them see how their role fits into the larger strategy.

Robotics and Automation

Robots have and will continue to enter the workforce in the next decade. Artificial intelligence will also help shape decision making and expedite processes that were once done by humans. Robots will create efficiencies and the ability to work long hours without breaks. Automation has been in place in manufacturing for a long time, and we will see this emerge into areas like transportation, health care, construction, agriculture, food preparation, military, mining, utilities, education, and others. After the 2020 Coronavirus Pandemic, robotic-driven health care will be an imperative. As robots are not infected with human viruses, they could save health-care lives on the front lines by administering tests and providing care while reserving human health care for more strategic functions.

A key issue and opportunity for the future of the workforce will be humans needed to code, repair, and manage (yes, manage) or oversee the robots and technology. As addressed in Chapter 3, robots will be flawed because they are built by flawed humans. Bias will exist. Sensors will misread information. It will be essential for all robotics to have human oversight and human override capability – this means human "safety" personnel. In this regard, much of the robotics and automation will be augmenting instead of replacing human functions. It will expedite what we can get done, but human oversight will still be required. We've already seen Amazon struggle with bias in its AI-driven recruitment tools. The data sets input favored men, so the outputs favored men. This was not intentional but was the outcome. Likewise, we've seen problems with robotics and automation like Tesla or Uber self-driven cars crashing when human drivers failed to course correct. This will become a bigger and bigger issue as more robotics are introduced into facets of work.

The role of Human Resources leaders will need to integrate with a new role of robotics and automation, beyond existing information technology. Additionally, cybersecurity over robotics will be heightened. The risk if a powerful robot is hacked could be significant if it is driving a truck, flying a plane, constructing a tall building, all of which could be turned into weapons and result in serious injuries and death. Likewise, a hacked robot nurse or doctor could dispense the wrong medication. Or, if you were a fan of the *Terminator* movies, a robot could try to destroy all humans. Science fiction is nearly a reality. The need for future workforces to factor in oversight functions and manual overrides and contingency plans will become central to managing risk. You can't keep piling it on to cybersecurity; this will become a separate function in the future. Consider the new facets of human work around artificial intelligence and robotics. Figure 5-2 illustrates the many issues intersecting with managing artificial intelligence and robotics in the workforce. Each component will be a role within the future workforce to avoid harmful unintended consequences. As much as some jobs will be replaced or augmented, new roles will be formed.

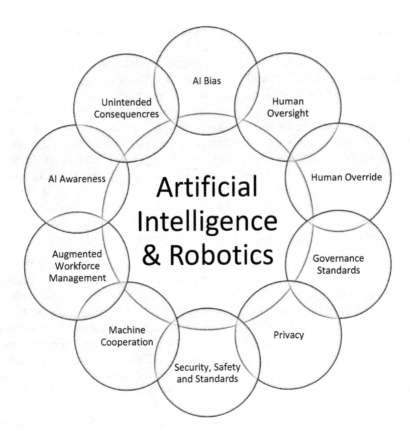

Figure 5-2. New Roles in Oversight of Artificial Intelligence and Robotics

Educating and Skill Building by Companies

Many Millennials are saddled with student loan debt. Gen Z is questioning the return on investment of how they acquire the skills they need. Most young people could learn a lot of what they need via online learning, which they adapted to during the 2020 Coronavirus Pandemic. And, the reality is, today's university graduates are often educated, but not properly skilled or trained for the jobs of the day. As the needs of companies change, companies may have to more actively participate in how young people are educated and trained to be prepared for the workforce they need.

Most companies have always had orientation and training programs, but this may be taken a step further in the decade ahead. Savvy companies are looking at how to partner with universities in creating more "practical" programs. For example, Google has partnered with universities to train students on what they need in order to work for Google. Other big tech companies have started to follow suit, and billionaire entrepreneurs such as Elon Musk have offered young people money (a "scholarship" of sorts) to skip college all together and get straight to work for his company. Some of the more practical college majors seeing a surge include construction management, agricultural engineering, food science, engineering (software, industrial, mechanical, chemical), management information systems, data or statistician, and others. After the 2020 Coronavirus Pandemic, many college-bound students are taking a gap year when facing online university experiences vs. in-person learning. Will they ultimately return to school or pursue other lines of education? Will they opt for less expensive online degrees while working and saving for their future? Will it have a long-lasting impact on traditional universities?

Many companies in need of data scientists, software engineers, solutions architects, product management, audit, and compliance could start to form programs on their corporate campuses to train and educate the students into their way of working to build their workforce of the future.

According to Bloomberg Next, only 35% of employers believe new recruits are well prepared with both technical skills and soft, relationship building, skills.

As demand-driven learning grows, partnering or investing to provide education for these in demand skills will grow for corporations. We see companies like KPMG building out state-of-the-art learning centers with hotel and resort-like amenities and campuses where they will provide training and education for their young recruits, as well as value-added education for clients. This style of education works well for Millennials and Gen Z and can be tailored to KPMG needs of the future before launching young people out into the workforce. It can also be used for continuing education as individuals move through their careers. Many companies are bypassing universities and going straight to high schools or technical colleges. Musk says when interviewing people to come work at Tesla, he's looking for their ability to solve problems not an Ivy League degree. He asks them to explain how they solved a problem to ensure they aren't taking credit for work someone else performed. A few ideas to consider from your boardroom as you contemplate the future of your workforce and skill building:

- Design training facilities for future generations. Dedicated training centers may help reduce labor costs by picking up talented students looking for an alternate path to a traditional university degree. This not only allows you to train your workforce but tap into a concept of loyalty that could be instilled in Gen Z before they are drowning in student debt.

- Adopt the virtual approach to continuous learning. Younger generations are more open to learning through virtual education. Consider investing in the development of training skills needed by younger people. This could range from specific on the job skills to life skills about staying healthy, managing their finances, and childcare – skills your workforce will need to be successful.

- Consider recruiting from alternative sources, tapping directly into high schools, trade schools, and two-year degrees vs. just the traditional four-year university. Skills are what you will need in the future, not just degrees.

- Partner with colleges, trade schools, or even high schools to provide training to potential recruits to start building the skill sets and creating the culture you want before onboarding future workers into your own training programs.

What Skills Will Matter in the Future?

New skills will be needed by everyone, including directors. Even for senior executives and board directors who are largely overseeing and providing direction for organization, they will need to learn and understand new technologies and cultural shifts to identify disruptive trends and needs of their organizations.

Additional skills from the workforce will be needed to compete in the next decade and beyond. Just a few of growth areas to consider in your workforce as well as your business offerings include:

- The experience society: As robots and technology take over more functions, humans will be seeking out enriching experiences. Companies that can deliver them better experiences both as a workforce and as consumers will see great opportunities and more competitive advantage.

  - This also means functions where humans benefit from the human contact or relationships could also become higher value: physicians and nurses, restaurants that continue to offer humans vs. robot servers, spas, health, wellness, tourism, and travel.

  - Managers will need to do the same to create a better experience for the workforce. How are you helping people deliver service and expertise throughout the organization?

- In the aftermath of the 2020 Coronavirus Pandemic, retail, dining, and in-person experiences are shifting to a blend of high value, worth going out to be in person and convenience factor, curbside pickup, or delivery. Balancing this blend and delivering high-value experiences for in-person activity will become a new business model.

- Creativity and innovation: Automated robots and tech driven by AI will do a lot of things, but it will not replace human creativity and innovation. Those who can think differently and strategically and push boundaries or help others to do this will continue to have value. Opportunities for creative thinking will increase as the reliance on automation and algorithms for mundane tasks increases. But it will require more focus and ability to harness that creative thinking. Companies may need to build out labs or spaces that foster creativity to tap into something that so far only humans can provide.

- Sales as a profession: Every company needs sales. And while algorithms and data crunching can help to monetize many things at a faster pace, most companies will still require some level of human relationship building to sell products and services either to consumers or businesses. While staple goods may not require cashiers in the future, higher-end products and services and certainly business-to-business services will still need a human touch. Relationships will become more valued in an automated society and those who possess the skill to build relationships will become the higher-value employees of the future. Many of the younger generations have not been taught how to communicate effectively off of technology. This will become a sought-after skill in the future. Much of this will stem from the ability to communicate and control your emotions, show empathy, and connect with others.

- Continuous learning: There is no question the ability to learn will be important. It's really that simple, adapt that way of thinking or become extinct. The ability to create education in a virtual environment will become a sought-after skill set. Understanding new technologies and their implications, both practical and theoretical, will be required by all. Virtual learning capabilities done on your time table will become a sought-after asset. Designing these programs will grow as a job function in the future.

- Judgment, ethics, and decision making: Also, important will be those who have the ability to make sound decisions based upon weighing facts from multiple viewpoints. The ability to gather and synthesize information and articulate a rational point of view will be in demand, particularly in the aftermath of "fake news," "deep fakes," and one-sided information permeating our culture. Machines will crank data based upon algorithms and deep learning capabilities, but humans will offer counsel to interpret it. Expect to see professional services grow that offer this very "human" ability to make decisions beyond programmed logic and algorithms. This area is where the "professions" or postgraduate education may become important. Lawyers and PhDs may become increasingly important in the roles that require sage counsel and wisdom through critical, compassionate, human, and balanced thinking.

- Human Resources and human capital: Human Resources will become central to a company's success. As the blend between automated work and human work becomes real, the need to effectively create a culture in an organization with clear strategy will increase. As millennials and Gen Z care far more about the culture of an organization than Boomers or Gen Xers, this will become a competitive differential for talented humans. The ability to lead, provide psychological support, and tap into the right skills of humans supported with the right tools will become an important strategic advantage to organizations large and small.

- Oversight, security, compliance, and privacy: These four areas will become dominant industries in the future. Artificial intelligence and robotics will require oversight. Some companies will do this internally and others will hire out professional oversight companies. The same will be true to comply with increasing complex global regulations over technology, data, and privacy. Consumers may turn to privacy companies to help them manage their own privacy in the future. These will be booming areas for career development.

- Programming and patching vulnerabilities: As everything we touch becomes connected to software and the Internet, the need for someone to oversee patching of vulnerabilities will grow. The need for programming, obviously, will also continue to grow; they will be augmented by automation.

- Construction and development: To retrofit our cities, roadways, buildings, and homes to meet the future demands of new energy sources and technology, those with expertise in construction and development will be in demand.

- Health care and wellness: Individuals who understand how to care for others and provide holistic health, wellness, as well as sickness care will become increasingly important. In the aftermath of the 2020 Pandemic, the need for robots to help with front-line diseases will be expanded, while humans will take on the careful role of overseeing robots and provide important human contact when needed, even if delivered through a machine. The entire industry will likely endure a complete paradigm shift in the near future so the ability to adapt and change is critical. Wellness was trending prior to the 2020 Coronavirus Pandemic. In the aftermath, self-care and attention to health and wellness will continue to be in demand from businesses and providers. Coupled with high-end experiences, expect to see hotels, spas, and salons morph into wellness centers leveraging a plethora of ways to experience self-care, pampering, and attention.

- Agriculture science: The need for fresh food and water will become increasingly important around the world. Those adept at building the facilities with innovative thinking will be in high demand.

- Energy, space, and engineering: The need to manage energy and navigate space will become hot areas of the future. Engineers who can help get there will also need policy and governance support to manage the myriad of complex legal issues that accompany these complex areas. Engineers will find themselves increasingly working with automation and augmented reality.

- Psychological support and human coaching. Humans will long for support to become better at running their lives. With more free time, as a result of more automation in the workforce, humans will have more time to pursue hobbies or relationships; humans may need help filling those gaps in a healthy way. Savvy companies will recognize the importance of providing this support.

Mental Health Will Become Critical to Company Leadership

In numerous studies, Millennials and Gen Z are found to be more depressed than Gen X or Baby Boomers at the same age. There are many possible reasons for this, ranging from increased pressure and time constraints throughout their youth, overstimulation by devices, YouTube, gaming, pop culture, social media, and fear for their future, which are all contributing factors. As robots and AI further commoditize human jobs, depression will likely increase.

How do companies prepare to lead, develop, and manage the mental health of their future workforce? Fostering and facilitating means of forming real connections, feeling a part of something bigger, and contributing will be critical to leading a successful workforce in the future. Providing support psychological services may be increasingly important.

Companies will need to put in place structure to help these younger generations connect with one another and engage in meaningful conversations to further their intellectual and relational capabilities. This will become essential to having a workforce that is mentally healthy and able to deliver the functions that will be needed by humans in the future. Companies may need to consider:

- Psychological support and services on staff and confidentially available for all employees to reduce time away from work and improve productivity.

- Psychology-based coaching for top performers to help them achieve at optimal performance.

- Social events intended to provide opportunities for comradery and formation of social friendships among young people may be needed on a regular basis. They may need ice breakers or tools to help interact and engage.

- Limit employee access to social media sites during the day to limit distraction and emotionally negative inputs.

- Monitor social media using artificial intelligence to look for trends of harassing behavior or depression among employees to head off problems before they become too big.

- Pep rally: Employees may need a pep rally of sorts to be excited about the work they are doing, the role the company has in the community, and feel a part of something bigger.

- Community service: This has long been a positive way to bring the workforce together and feel like they are doing something positive — finding more community-based service projects and investing time, money, and resources may go a long way in building a solid and happier workforce of the future.

- Utilize software to monitor employee emails and interactions to look for signs of depression and intervene in a productive and confidential manner.

Will the Sharing Economy Last?

The sharing economy and concept of earning extra money through side gigs using something you already have (your car, your home, an office space, or even a talent) created micro-entrepreneurs across generations. While the gig economy has been a great success for the individual, the company platforms providing it have not yet seen widespread profitability. For example, as of early 2020, Uber, Airbnb, and WeWork were all not profitable. Uber was losing billions per quarter, though their CEO said that is coming to an end and they will be profitable by the end of 2020. But, that was before the 2020 Coronavirus Pandemic. According to Forbes, in its initial public offering, it raised $9 billion, which means it likely isn't sustainable to continue to lose billions each quarter. Statistically, they lose 25 cents on every dollar it brings in. After the 2020 Coronavirus Pandemic, even with radical changes, profitability is likely not attainable in 2020. Airbnb lost $322 million over the first nine months of 2019. The board wanted to know why costs are growing faster than revenue when an IPO was looming on the horizon. Will people return to renting homes vs. hotels with health and sanitation standards after the pandemic? Time will tell, but these models may simply not be sustainable, or the approach may have to change for it to work into the future.

These companies were innovative, creating the opportunity to earn money by providing an "on-demand" service. Consumers love it, there's no question about it. But can it be done profitably? As discussed in Chapter 1, a problem for these companies is that they scaled quickly by breaking rules. They didn't necessarily pay payroll taxes for drivers or buy taxi medallions that were required by local municipalities. They didn't charge local tourism taxes and don't comply with health ordinances for providing hotel services.

If these companies have to play by the same rules as every other company, will they make it? What other solutions will appear for the gig economy workers? We know the concept works. Workers like the opportunity. Consumers like the service. But it may be subject to some changes and shifts in the future. Does it need to be integrated into companies with a cost structure for those "extra" expenses as an add-on? Can it be added on profitably? Can it be rolled out inside existing profitable companies to tap into the opportunity, but managed from the outset more effectively?

Companies like Upwork help connect freelancers with companies who need their services. Angie's List, Craigslist, Etsy, and eBay all help peer-to-peer transactions. Rent the Runway gives women the chance to wear the latest designer styles without the price tag. Angie's List took 21 years to become profitable. eBay has investors worried about the future.

The concept works and it may be a solution to future workforce shortages or needs. In fact, many companies find contract or temporary workers an effective solution to expanding the size of their full-time workforce when costs like payroll taxes, medical benefits, and management are added into the mix. For companies needing services like drivers or freelance writers or designers, the sharing economy is certainly a good option. And for people who want to rent a home or an outfit for a night, it's a nice service. But will the business model be able to sustain long-term losses? What happens when they have to cover costs they circumvented in the beginning?

There could be good opportunities to replicate these models with sharing platforms and technology becoming easier to implement now that the road has been paved for consumers to understand how it works.

Boards should consider their workforce needs and how the gig economy could benefit it in the future. Do you build something yourself, partner with an existing player, or buy up a company for the technology, or do you just watch from the sidelines to see what happens? It will all impact the overall culture and attitude toward the workforce.

The American Dream 2.0

The future of work for many could be in owning their own businesses. According to Forbes, Gen Z are 55% more likely to start a business than millennials. According to Millennial Branding, a study shows that 72% of Gen Z high school students say they want to start a business. Franchising has long been a solution for those who don't feel they get a fair shake in corporations. For many women and minorities, this has been the path to becoming a self-made millionaire. Women constitute 35% of all franchise owners in the United States. Nearly half of all new franchisees are women. Small business owners know the secret. When you own your own business, you have the ability to create a vision, be a part of something bigger, and control your own destiny and schedule. These are all characteristics that fit the next generation's definition of success.

Even large companies have seen the value of helping their employees start businesses. Amazon recognized its needs for more local delivery companies. So, it offered employees $10,000 to go start a company that would supply

Amazon in an area of need. Expect to see more companies looking at their supply chain and considering how they might help create the regional or local supply chain they need vs. sourcing it from unpredictable vendors and new variables in global trade. Tapping into small businesses to support your organization's supply chain can boost your workforce, boost your supply chain, and tap into fresh and innovative ideas.

There are also opportunities for companies to be a part of the entrepreneurship trend by supporting community incubators, partnering with entrepreneurs, and even creating franchises for important vertical components of your industry. Consider sponsoring entrepreneurial contests for businesses you need in your supply chain. Additionally, startup and emerging companies can be great sources to acquire innovative products and services vs. investing in internal research and development (R&D). Internal R&D is often plagued with a "not invented here" syndrome which limits outside-the-box thinking. This is why many companies look to entrepreneurs to fuel their innovation programs. Whether you are adding to your supply chain or searching for the next innovative trend to leverage in your company, the new American Dream is something worth supporting for a generation more open than ever before.

Most local areas have an economic development center which would gladly partner with corporations in growing the entrepreneurial base in the community. While it has often been in tech, it can also be in other aspects of supply chain that may become hard to source in the future.

Boards should consider how they can potentially utilize startup companies, franchising or help employees start companies to fill gaps anticipated in their supply chain.

Suburban, Urban, and Rural Transformations

As Millennials and Gen Z seek more affordable housing and closer proximity to enjoyable life experiences, there are opportunities for companies to help build out new communities and campuses in these growing areas. For those who stay in urban areas, needs will also change. Companies may need to be aware of an increasing desire to work from home as traffic and health safety become bigger issues for commuting in large urban areas. Companies should carefully consider how lifestyle demands will change in urban, suburban, and rural areas to capitalize on opportunities. In the aftermath of the 2020 Coronavirus Pandemic, many companies will also adopt more remote work options which could facilitate moves for many outside of urban hubs. It may also prompt companies to relocate big office centers outside of urban areas that can be shut down for a month or longer.

Rural communities will need access to high-speed Internet, new energy sources, and ways of connecting. They may need driverless car services to cover long distances without a lot of traffic. They may become locations for building out facilities to serve localized supply chains and developing lower cost workforces.

Big urban hubs will require easy access to fundamentals like housing, food, clean water, and transportation. Shared automated transportation will increase out of necessity, but likely morph to allow for long-term social distancing. The cost for cities to provide services in a social distancing era will increase, ultimately increasing the cost of living in urban areas.

Suburban areas with lower costs of living will mimic the offerings of big cities with a balance between the convenience and experience offerings of major cities with the slower pace and sense of community in rural areas.

In all settings, companies need to be prepared for a workforce living in diverse environments and provide for remote work. As the 2020 Coronavirus Pandemic made clear, events beyond the control of companies or even governments can suddenly impact the ability for business as usual. Providing for remote and virtual work to continue in any situation will become the new normal. This will help in reducing unnecessary travel, reduce costs, and become a bigger motivator. Process and accountability mechanisms for virtual work will become a part of work life as you need to attract talent.

Working from home eliminates commuting, which for many could be up to an hour or more each way a day – that's a lot of time for exercise, family, meditation, thinking, health, and wellness – all of which we now need more than ever. The future of service workers likely involves a blend of some in-office socialization, workshopping, collaborating, and meeting combined with at-home or remote work. This will allow companies to tap into talent wherever they may live. It can also reduce costly office space by designing spaces for work that is done together, not alone. While Boomers and Gen Xers have long valued the prized corner office as a status symbol of success, future generations will value the flexibility of working remotely and pride themselves on their productivity and ability to have a better quality of life as a result. Boards, too, may look at more remote cycles to their structure to reduce travel costs and expense of meetings and increase productivity of decision making vs. sitting in person in long meetings.

Tools that allow leaders and managers to hold workers accountable and facilitate productive work across locations will be worth the investment. Providing employees company devices and connections will be essential to security management.

Additionally, process improvement techniques that track processes for efficiency will see a migration from the manufacturing floor into remote work environments – how can things like meetings with a lot of people be done more efficiently and how can tasks be streamlined? For example, if the purpose is primarily to present information, why not record it and verify that each essential person watches or listens to the entire session? Then allow for group chatting of questions to facilitate accountability vs. trying to manage more than ten people on a call. You don't need to know who has a hard stop at the top of the hour if it is prerecorded so you might eliminate the never ending "who's just joined?" cycle at the beginning of calls with a lot of people.

Conversations can only occur with a small number of people – usually 3 or 4 maximum. Instead of spending time in mind-numbing meetings, how can a service-based workforce be turned into something more productive? I have spent years applying Six Sigma techniques to professional services to reduce costs and increase profitability – the entire service sector may see this as a future trend.

Consider carefully as a board how you develop a workforce in urban, suburban, and rural areas. What types of workers can you attract from these areas? How can they support your future needs?

Tone at the Top – Culture Assessments

History often repeats itself. Many Baby Boomers believe they were no different than Millennials of today in demanding societal shifts and changes in the way we work and live. But as Boomers grew into adulthood, they began to value "things" and "prestige" as their driver and motivator. Millennials may follow a similar pattern, though forever plagued by social media may continue to demand a sense of meaning and want to curate a version of themselves that is shared with others as their "status symbol." Mired in the belief that the economy could collapse again and again, they will shy away from valuing things vs. experiences.

Gen Xers followed the rules the Boomers created in the workplace and mirrored Boomers' desire for luxury and things as a status symbol. Gen Z, the children of Gen Xers, likewise want to follow a path and rules to success, but value authenticity and meaning as their status symbol. The convergence of these generations in the workforce creates new demands on corporate culture to drive behavior and results.

Boards need to understand the culture of the organization and what is driving and motivating top performers. Boards also need to understand the driving forces of the workforce it will need. While the board is increasingly taxed with pressing issues, every few years, it should undertake a cultural assessment of the organization and a clear reflection to define the future workforce.

There are three primary ways to conduct a cultural assessment: hiring a consulting firm with their proprietary methods, hiring an academician with an anthropological approach, or conducting a self-assessment.

Proprietary Methods – Hire a Consulting Firm

There are many consultants that have developed a framework for culture assessment. Many of them are filled with catch phrases and buzzwords they try to coin. There are big powerhouse recruiters and the big consulting firms all offer high-priced proprietary culture assessments. There are many boutique consultants and firms that can also help evaluate culture at a more reasonable price. Depending upon the size of your organization and how broad the scope of the assessment needed, you may not need a high-priced culture assessment to understand what's actually going on, but you do need to pay attention to culture and every few years an outside assessment can give you a good refreshed look at how culture impacts your ability to meet your stakeholder goals.

Hiring an outside firm to provide a culture assessment can provide valuable insights, but there are alternative approaches.

Anthropological Approach of Culture

Another more academically driven culture assessment that could be equally useful is an anthropological approach, which factors in the following:

- Norms
  - What is expected
  - Chain of command, respect
  - Dress code, attire
- Languages
  - Jargon
  - Internal acronyms
- Heroes and Heroines
  - Role models
  - Visionaries
- Customs
  - Arriving early/staying late
  - Work–life balance
- Myths
  - Shared stories told to newcomers

- Mores
  - Right or wrong behavior
- Ceremonies and Celebrations
  - What is measured and valued gets done
  - How is it celebrated
- Symbols
  - Events and things with special meaning

Typically, a university professor will specialize in delivering this more academically driven type of cultural assessment, though caution should be given to make sure the outcomes are practical recommendations for implementation. This might be a nice alternative to the traditional "consulting"-driven model and give you a fresh perspective of how the organization operates. As you approach culture assessments, alternating the types of assessments you use can provide insightful comparisons. In other words, don't use the same consultant or same methodology every time you do a culture assessment.

Self-Assessment

A final option is to engage in your own self-assessment of culture as a board member. This comes from getting into the field, talking with people, and looking for a few key indicators:

- Evaluate and understand how new employees at all levels are onboarded to the company.
- Gauge openness within leadership.
- Evaluate incentives throughout the organization – top to bottom.
- Observe teams in action.
  - Do they respect each other, do they relate, and how do they perform cohesively?
- Ask questions of random employees.
  - What went well or not well last year?
  - What were the cringeworthy moments?
  - What would you change if you could?
  - How do we learn from our mistakes?

- What is holding us back?
- If you could start your department over with a blank slate, what would you do?

- Discuss the questions at the end of this chapter with your board and be mindful of the role of culture.

A self-assessment can be informal, as simple as a few board members taking time to talk with employees, particularly those at the front line who sell your product or service. This is something you can do on a regular basis to augment and supplement a more formal study.

Conclusion

Understanding future generations and the trends impacting the workforce on your culture will be increasingly important as the needs of all companies shift and evolve with technology and new demands. Culture is what sets the tone of the organization. If it's broken, you will need help to fix it. It can't be done internally if it's broken. Find a good advisor or consulting partner to help you assess it and course correct. It also helps you see the importance of psychology in the future of managing the workforce.

If it's working, carefully nurture it and monitor incentives so you don't damage the culture that has been built. Revisit the subject at least biannually to ensure your culture and your organization are prepared for new generations of leaders and that you are cultivating the human capital you will need to survive disruption. As the way we all work morphs in the aftermath of the 2020 Coronavirus Pandemic, creating and sustaining a culture that drives toward business goals will be more important than ever.

Discussion Questions for the Boardroom

1. How will your company be prepared to introduce robotics or automation in the workforce?

2. How do you attract and retain talent from Millennials and Gen Z?

3. How do you create a culture that is sustainable?

4. How do you value the culture?

5. How are you cultivating leaders from younger generations and preparing them for the future?

6. Do you partner with universities or schools to help provide training?

7. How will you meet future workforce demands for flexibility and remote work environments?

8. Do you think the sharing economy will continue? How does it impact your company?

9. Can you tap into entrepreneurial opportunities through incubators and accelerators?

10. What about supporting entrepreneurship in areas that could support your local supply chain needs?

11. How will you address mental health issues of the future?

12. Is Human Resources given enough authority to create the culture you need?

13. How do you regularly assess the culture to know if it will sustain you into the future?

14. How are you identifying the skills matrix you will need in the future and how that is met across your organization?

15. How does the c-suite work together to create a culture that is healthy for the organization to achieve its objectives? Is this ever discussed?

16. How is your supply chain impacted by cultural shifts? Do you need a more regional or local supply chain that can be provided by younger generations?

Environmental and Social Governance

We are in one of the most divided times in history; how do we balance out so many competing needs and be good stewards to benefit all stakeholders?

Environmental and social governance, referred to now as "ESG," has become a hot topic in boardroom education. In brief, ESG means our society as a whole expects corporations to be responsible and accountable to not just shareholders but all stakeholders (employees, vendors, customers, strategic partners, and the community as a whole). It means boards may be held to a standard in the future for how well the corporation cares about the stakeholders impacted by it vs. just financial value to shareholders. This means boards must care about what matters to stakeholders – "Stakeholder Values."

According to NACD' s 2019 survey, ESG is becoming commonplace in the boardroom, although not "high value" like other areas such as audit, succession planning, and growth strategies. Nearly 80% of public company boards now engage with ESG issues including linkages of Stakeholder Values to strategy and risk. Also, discussions with investors focus on elements related to human capital and diversity. But what does all of that really mean?

J. C. Wolfe, *Disruption in the Boardroom*, https://doi.org/10.1007/978-1-4842-6159-0_6

In 2018, Larry Fink, CEO of BlackRock, wrote a letter to other CEOs to pursue a purpose beyond profits and consider all stakeholders. He called for purpose and profit, exemplifying a new era for corporations in an era of corporate social responsibility. CEOs from Apple, JP Morgan, and many other high-profile companies chimed in to agree.

This chapter will briefly address what these issues are and how the board is expected to address them. Most of these issues deal with the concept of "tone at the top," meaning the board along with the CEO help set the tone or culture of the organization. All of these ESG issues deal with culture. What is valued in the company? How do people treat each other? How do you succeed and get ahead?

While some argue this is all about "political correctness," it's really about the workplace environment. It's also about how your company leads in a digital age where any off-color comment caught on camera can go viral and ruin your personal reputation along with damage to your company's brand. It could be a senior leader or even a counter worker at a location, regardless it reflects badly on the whole company when it goes viral. Remember in 2018 when a Philadelphia Starbucks employee kicked out two African Americans waiting for a friend but who hadn't purchased anything? The Starbucks CEO shut down all stores in the United States for racial bias education as a result. Was that overkill or an important connecting point with the public? Was the outcome a more favorable outlook on Starbucks by customers?

It's a difficult time to manage these issues at the top. Failure to address perceived failures anywhere in the organization can illustrate a lack of sensitivity to issues important to many of your stakeholders. And, yet there is a point where leaders must be practical and realistic about succumbing to an angry Twitter mob and the dangerous precedent that can set.

This is not easy for leaders. For almost all of the ESG issues, there are divergent viewpoints and research and statistics on which those viewpoints rely. In the boardroom, there is a responsibility to hear all of those viewpoints, but then make appropriate decisions about the culture of the company to best meet the needs of your stakeholders: employees, customers, vendors, strategic partners, shareholders, and the community you serve. Let's look at a few of the bigger issues, and then I'll close with an exercise boards can do to develop their own point of view around Stakeholder Values.

Leadership in a Digital Age

On April 10, 2017, after a paying customer was dragged off a United Airlines flight in Chicago kicking and screaming with a bloody head, the CEO of the company tweeted:

> *This is an upsetting event to all of us here at United. I apologize for having to accommodate these customers. Our team is moving with a sense of urgency to work with the authorities and conduct our own detailed review of what happened. We are also reaching out to this passenger to talk directly with him and further address and resolve this situation.*

He was blasted immediately on Twitter for not recognizing the gravity of the situation or taking responsibility for the fact that a paying passenger was dragged off of one of his airplanes so his flight attendants could get to their next flight. The airline had prioritized their own logistics problem over passenger needs and safety. In his tweet, Munoz thought he was defending his employees and their position. In the viral social media world, he was seen as a jerk out of touch with what it is to be an average passenger on his planes. Two decades ago, there would not be a way for that message to circulate the flying public so quickly. If a reporter didn't report on it, it would simply go away. But today, this story and others can live on in social media purgatory. CEOs need to be careful about their use of social media when we live in a time where someone somewhere will likely be offended about almost anything.

Some do it right. Tim Cook, of Apple, for example, has been praised for how he interacts with Apple customers and tweets about it – showing genuine concern for his customers and prioritizing customer service. Virgin CEO, Richard Branson, also focuses on engaging with his constituents vs. selling. Elon Musk has also been effective at answering complaints or responses to customers. Airbnb CEO, Brian Chesky, has been known to ask for ideas and crowdsource new ways to do things through Twitter.

Social media can have strategic purpose and achieve important goals, carefully managed, but the downside must always be considered. You would not give a press conference without carefully scripting your remarks and being prepared for how you will answer questions. The same diligence, if not more, should be applied to social media because it can be amplified so quickly and is never really erased.

Additionally, almost anywhere we go, cameras are watching, cell phones can be turned into recording devices, and everyone wants to post a popular video. If you are a high-profile CEO or director, be careful what you say and do in public. It can easily be used against you. This is simply the time in which we now live. A heightened level of awareness is critical. The bottom line: be careful what you say and do in public and in the boardroom, monitor your own social media, and track what your CEO and other executives are doing on social media.

Environmental Issues and Climate Change

Companies are responding to demands to be good stewards of the planet, be conscientious about environmental issues, and think about their use of energy. From a marketing perspective, "being green" has been popular since the 1980s. McDonald's, for example, stopped using styrofoam boxes and instead switched to environmentally friendly cardboard boxes. Also, in the 1980s, Chevron launched a series of expensive television and print ads to convince the public it was environmentally friendly. Today, marketing about "green" or environmentally conscious initiatives certainly is a winner and sometimes required. BP spent nearly 100 million in advertising in just four months following its 2010 oil spill in the Gulf of Mexico to reshape public opinion. But it's more than just public relations, the demands by the public at large to be environmentally conscious are very real.

This means the conversation in the boardroom about the environmental impact of the company has become increasingly important. As referenced in Chapter 3, Microsoft's announcement at Davos 2020 that it would "erase" its carbon footprint by developing technology to reverse the effects sends a clear message that companies are striving to demonstrate their commitment to not only reduce their impact on the environment but erase it. Yet, just a few weeks later, it became clear fulfilling on that promise may be difficult. When a facility in North Dakota ran short of energy from its local provider, Microsoft flipped on diesel generators to power its campus on a very cold day. In response, Microsoft's chief environmental officer, Lucas Joppa, said "no one should have their head in the sand about the difficulty of the energy transformation for a global economy." Many other companies like Johnson & Johnson and Pernod Ricard have made public pledges to achieve goals for emissions reduction or use of renewable energy. Goals might include use of energy, water, reducing the carbon footprint, sustainable production practices, and waste reduction, among others.

Directors should discuss these issues and develop clear points of view around the company's position related to climate change and what steps, if any, it is taking to address demands from the public or respond to government treaties and policies addressing climate change. And, if it makes pledges for public relations reasons, there needs to be a clear strategy to achieve those goals.

Despite the many speeches at the annual World Economic Forum about Climate Change, companies have not yet changed their policies when it comes to private jets or flying employees around the world. A Swedish university study called out celebrities who call for the need to address the climate crisis but are themselves "super emitters" owning and traveling on private jets. Microsoft founder, Bill Gates, took 59 flights in 2017 traveling more than 200,000 miles on a private jet. Jeff Bezos flies a Gulfstream G650ER that seats eight people. Mark Cuban owns three jets plus two 757s to fly around his

Dallas Mavericks team. He also charters out a private 767. Elon Musk flies a Gulfstream G650ER. And Google founders, Sergey Brin and Larry Page, own a fleet of planes through a holding company. Take Davos 2020, for example. For this four-day conference, nearly 600 private jets arrived to bring in the billionaires and world leaders, a number that does not take into account public figures such as presidents and prime ministers. The World Economic Forum says it offsets the carbon emitted by funding projects that seek to reduce emissions. However, this logic falls flat. It's a nice talking point, but that practice does not eliminate the carbon emitted from each private jet. This type of scrutiny is front and center on boardroom behavior. This is the fundamental example of needing to "practice what you preach."

So far, high-profile companies and their leaders aren't ditching the jet lifestyle. With the increased attention on climate change and how companies are stewards of the planet, expect to see more scrutiny of personal use of jets and how companies make decisions to put people on the road vs. using technology for meetings. As boards address environmental issues, they need to be prepared for a realistic look at what the company is doing and what senior leaders and board members are doing that could be called upon as hypocritical. None of this means you can't still use the company jet, but recognize that if you do, you need to be careful how you message the company's environmental initiatives because in an environment that quickly calls out behavior of those with wealth and power, you need to be prepared.

Likewise, in the aftermath of the 2020 Coronavirus Pandemic, companies will be evaluated for how they stepped up and did their part to support employees and the health and wellbeing of the country and the world.

At its 2019 annual meeting, Amazon's board recommended a vote against a climate change proposal calling for the company to report how it is "planning for disruptions posed by climate change, and how Amazon is reducing its company-wide dependence on fossil fuels." The proposal, put forth by roughly 8000 employees, received just 30% support from shareholders, but the issue remained of paramount importance to Amazon's workers. In September, after Amazon employees prepared to join a large protest over the tech industry's perceived inaction on climate, the company announced that it would join an effort to reduce climate impact. Broad groups of stakeholders will likely continue to make ESG demands of management and director "mindshare" in 2020 and immediately beyond. Boards should ensure that their companies have identified the most relevant stakeholder groups and that they have a robust strategy to engage with them.

What is your policy on being a good steward of the environment? Beyond talking points, how do you back it up with consistent actions? And, when you can't, how are you prepared to defend or communicate your position?

#MeToo, Sexual Harassment, and Related Issues

The last few years have seen the fall of powerhouse media moguls such as Harvey Weinstein, Matt Lauer, Less Moonves, and Charlie Rose, to name just a few. The gauntlet has been thrown down that women will no longer tolerate sexually hostile work environments or harassment from top bosses. Boards, too, have responded by firing these powerful men, signaling a zero-tolerance policy. While many women have celebrated this long sought-after success and are thankful the light has finally been shined on egregious and bad behavior, it has now left some important questions for both men and women in the workplace.

How do we create a safe space to build important friendships and collegial relationships that are important to career growth? The reality is that many women need relationships with more senior men (as well as women) to ascend to higher positions. It's important to discuss the board's viewpoint about some of these issues and the position on critical matters that will be faced in the future.

While the light was turned on to this, there remain concerns of volatile or uncomfortable work environments. Uber employee, Susan Fowler, wrote a blog about the "frat boy" culture at Uber, which was addressed through a cultural study and has now become a vocal advocate for women in the workplace, working at *The New York Times*. Google employees protested its handling of sexual harassment claims in November of 2018 saying that one of Google's leaders, Andy Rubin, walked away with $90 million in an exit package despite finding the sexual misconduct claims against him credible. Nearly 20% of their workforce around the world walked out in protest.

The demand by women for a zero-tolerance approach to senior executives who abuse their power is not likely to go away. But what really matters is addressing the culture that allows this to continue. All of the ESG topics relate to culture that is set at the top. In the boardroom you decide whether the senior executives are held to the same standards as everyone else. You decide if they are given golden parachutes amid evidence of abusive behavior. There may be good contractual or other reasons to allow an executive an easy way out, but the impact on the culture must be considered. As you address these issues, there are surely policy positions you can put in place to ensure everyone has an anonymous channel to voice concerns and for claims to be properly independently investigated. The HR and legal departments need to work together to provide that framework to ensure employee safety. It starts with candid conversations among board members and the senior executives, continues with arriving at clearly defined viewpoints, and ends with policies that are fairly enforced. Consider these questions:

- How do you ensure you have a corporate culture where women are not directly or indirectly pressured into sexual relationships with men higher on the management chain? Or, for that matter, anywhere in the company?

- To be fair, how do you ensure women don't abuse their power toward more junior men in the organization as well?

- How do you protect whistleblowers?

- Do you monitor social media and recruitment sites for indicators that your workplace could have a hostile work environment?

- How do you create a safe space for all employees to report inappropriate behavior?

- Do you have cameras to capture workplace interactions and verify the veracity of statements made?

- Do you have clear policies about travel by coworkers to eliminate the propensity for an inappropriate relationship to form?

- How do you ensure that there are positive and productive mentoring relationships to help both men and women develop important connections to more senior people and advance their careers?

Diversity

Diversity in the workplace has been a hot topic for the last two decades. At the boardroom level, there continues to be a drive for more parity among women and men and minorities during board refreshment to ensure diverse perspectives are heard. Most companies embraced this concept years ago and have built important programs to provide workplace diversity employment and retention practices, as well as cultural awareness.

The Women's Advocacy Group, 2020 Women on Boards, said that by the end of 2019, women held more than 20% of the board seats at the top 3000 publicly traded companies. The number is a significant increase from 15% in 2016, when Equilar began tracking the metrics. Sixty percent of women in board positions took the job when new seats were created by expanding boards, not by replacing male directors. However, one-third of companies still only have one woman on the board. According to the NACD annual report, more women are joining boards; however, progress is slow.

There is no shortage of groups and organizations dedicated to helping women get their seat at the table with a goal of parity among male and female directors. California and Illinois have passed legislation requiring companies to appoint women to their boards or face fines. In Europe, the EU Commission approved a 40% quota of female nonexecutive directors on company boards by 2020. While there isn't any federal legislation currently pending in the United States, recruiters say there is definitely a push for it right now. The reality is what is mandated gets done, but some are concerned that's not the best way to do it. Some fear that the women on those boards will not be treated the same or have the same power as the men on the board. And others just feel quotas are insulting. "This legislation is, to me, insulting," Lucy Dunn, President and CEO of the Orange County Business Council, said in a statement after the vote. Others cite that what gets measured and tracked gets done.

In 2019, Forbes issued its list of innovative leaders that included only one woman. They were quickly blasted for that misstep. Whether this is making a difference or not is also debatable. In France, Germany, and the Netherlands (all of which have a quota a system), the percentage of senior management jobs held by women has not really changed and the pay gap did not decrease either, according to Forbes.

Whatever your opinion may be on this issue, it is likely that more quotas will come until there is parity of women and men on boards. Diversity of the workforce will not go away as the workforce of the future shifts and changes. Like all of these cultural issues, it is important to have a clear viewpoint as a board and continually revisit your position.

Another important element of diversity that is emerging in the boardroom is diversity of thought. According to an ISS (Institutional Shareholder Services) study, critical director skills are missing from company boards. For the last few decades, most boards seek out a CEO or CFO of a similarly sized company to serve on the board. While that made sense two decades ago, it simply doesn't anymore. There are too many new issues that require specialized knowledge and experiences; all of which have been discussed in this book: changing business models, new technologies, cybersecurity, the future of work, societal shifts, and environmental, political, and social issues that require more than just expertise as the CEO or CFO. Most CEOs are charismatic leaders who rise to the top through adept relationship building and savvy decision making. CFOs understand the complexities of finance and audit. Both skills are certainly still needed in the boardroom. But not every seat should be filled with that profile.

When it comes to diversity of gender or race, the practicality is that there is a small pool of individuals who check the gender or race box desired while also checking the ex-CEO or CFO box of a similarly sized company. Accordingly, this contributes to the lack of diversity of race, gender, and thought in the boardroom. The push to add new skill sets in the boardroom as well as gender and racial diversity will continue in the decade ahead. By changing the skill sets sought after, boards may inherently widen the pool to allow for more gender and racial diversity.

Political Polarization and Activism in the Workplace

Decades ago, the general rule was to not discuss politics in the workplace. Policies might be discussed if relevant to the matter at hand, but personal politics was, well, personal. That is no longer true. In fact, employees become so vocal about their politics that at some companies, they revolt if the company takes a political position they don't like. Many employees believe it is their duty to hold their company accountable when the actions differ from their personal political views. There is a sharp departure on this philosophy between Millennials and the prior Baby Boomer and Gen Xer generations.

Google, for example, had an employee protest over the company contract with the Pentagon to develop artificial intelligence for drone video analysis. Senior executives said that it was a $9 million project that could lead to billions of dollars in cloud work for the company. More than 4000 staff signed a petition to stop it and some actually quit. Thousands walked off the job worried that the technology could be used to kill people. Many argue the technology would save lives by improving the functionality of the AI. But the project was a public relations nightmare and the company ultimately caved. Google is still, however, working with China on artificial intelligence, known as Dragonfly. The program could help the Chinese government censor broad categories of information through the government-censored Internet, particularly those in categories related to human rights, democracy, health, religion, and peaceful protest. Employees also protested this project, but it was not cancelled by executives. So, Google continues to help China censor the Internet and violate human rights, but it is no longer helping the US government improve AI accuracy in drone technology that could save lives in the future.

Employees at Amazon, Facebook, Google, and Microsoft also all pledged to walk out in September of 2018 in a climate change protest in order to pressure their companies to do more on climate change. Most of these companies cite some changes they are making as a result.

While it can be argued that these companies have a largely liberal employee base and these were essentially liberal positions, it raises an important question, "how do you manage political polarization in the workplace?" Google was facing a class action lawsuit by former Google employees claiming discrimination on political bias against conservative viewpoints. The judge allowed the case to move forward, but the employees ultimately dismissed the case without a clear reason why. Facebook has been targeted under the "cancel culture" of celebrities because they believe their policies on political ads support conservative agendas.

The board will have to address the culture and the policies of the organization to handle the political polarization and activism of employees. Whatever your personal position, the board needs to clearly determine how it understands Stakeholder Values and when and if it will cave to "cancel culture" pressure.

Will this type of employee revolt be tolerated, encouraged, successful? I have talked to many CEOs who understand that all political viewpoints need to be heard and understood to make savvy decisions. Shutting down any one viewpoint does not lead to better outcomes, particularly if you alienate half of your customers in the process. It is dangerous for boards to respond to extremist demands from their employees without a clear strategy behind it.

Do you allow or encourage employees to voice their political views? Do you encourage respect among differing viewpoints and suggest that employees focus on work while at work? That unless their job is to address a policy issue, that they focus on what they are doing? Will that work when we have two generations that very much want to feel they work for a company they believe in and is doing the right thing? Would it harm you if a big part of your workforce walked out because of a company position on a political issue?

Some companies may not be facing these extreme issues like Google or Facebook, but it's worth a conversation over your next board dinner. What is your policy on politics in the workplace? To understand how you may have to adapt to address this issue, you need to fully understand your company's stakeholders. Not every company will be the same, so there is not a one-size-fits-all solution.

Stakeholder Engagement Assessment

To evaluate how you engage stakeholders, take time to talk with your fellow board members. Use the following exercise as a guide:

Stakeholder Engagement Plan – Boardroom Exercise

1. Define your stakeholders, who are they, what subsets of these groups do you serve?

    a. Employees

    b. Customers

    c. Vendors

    d. Strategic partners

    e. Communities you serve

2. What do they value, what matters to them, what concerns them, how do you meet their needs and values? Consider the following areas:

   - Environmental

     - Climate change

     - Carbon footprint of the company

     - Natural resource management

     - Waste management

     - Biodiversity

     - Animal wellbeing and testing

     - Natural and man-made disaster responses

     - Sustainability programs

   - Social and Political

     - Human rights and supply chain

     - Labor relations

     - Employee diversity and inclusion

     - Product safety and quality

     - Future of work

     - Employee health and safety

     - Pandemic preparedness

     - Employee crisis management

3. How do you meet the needs of your stakeholder values?

4. How do you incorporate this into your boardroom discussions?

5. When making decisions, do you ask how this impacts your stakeholders and what matters to them?

6. Do you survey your stakeholders through an outside party?

   a. Consider using a 360-survey approach with customers, employees, and vendors to better understand what issues they face and how your actions impact them.

7. What happens if you anger these groups?

8. What happens if you don't meet their needs?

9. What happens if you mobilize these groups to work toward your goals and objectives?

10. How will you respond in a crisis if you violate a key stakeholder value?

11. How do these values align with your business strategy?

12. How can you improve connection points and engagement with stakeholders?

13. Do you cave to an angry group? What will keep you from being a continual target to anyone who doesn't like something you do as an organization?

14. Do you allow politics in the workplace? What are the pros and cons of that choice?

15. How do you keep a pulse on what matters to your stakeholders?

16. What's your crisis response plan if a stakeholder group publicly attacks you?

Conclusion

Taking time to understand your stakeholders will become a critical role of the board in the future. This isn't something you can outsource to a consultant, you need to take the time to discuss these issues and listen to stakeholders in order to make the sage decisions that will be required of boards in an increasingly complex time.

This is one of those issues where we will need moral courage from our leaders. It's easier to just give in to an angry mob, but not always the right thing to do. Having principles driven by ESG pressures is important. But the real test is whether as a board you stand by those principles when it is not convenient or easy. To make tough decisions, you need to understand your stakeholders before you find yourself facing a disruptive event.

Discussion Questions for the Boardroom

Additional ESG culture questions to consider:

1. What is your company policy about the CEO and directors on social media?

2. How do you ensure the culture provide a safe space for all employees free from unwanted sexual advances, particularly by senior executives or those who have more power in the organization?

3. What are you doing to achieve more diversity and parity among your executive team and board?

4. Is there a company position on climate change?

5. How do you address employee cultural concerns for recycling, sustainability in decision making, and purchasing power?

6. How do you evaluate your use of energy and future energy?

7. Are your buildings and facilities designed for the future?

8. How do you create a culture of inclusion and watch for unintended bias?

9. How are you considering diversity of thought and experience on your board?

10. How do you ensure employees can safely report inappropriate sexual behavior or advances?

11. Do you have a zero-tolerance policy? What happens if it's a much beloved or successful executive?

12. How do you manage extreme political views and activism in the workplace?

13. In the boardroom, do you consider multiple political points of view when making decisions that are impacted by policies?

14. How do you help set the cultural tone?

15. How do you assess risks of environmental and social issues?

The Future of the Boardroom

The old structure of the board will not work in the decade ahead. No one likes change. But disruption is the new normal, which means the boardroom must change with it.

This chapter provides a practical framework for managing a vast new world of technology, cybersecurity, societal shifts, and unexpected health pandemics and a new structure for good governance and oversight from the boardroom.

An article in Forbes early into 2020 highlighted that "corporate governance is going to have to change." It cited the Blue Ribbon Commission report from the National Association of Corporate Directors ("Fit for the Future: An Urgent Imperative for Board Leadership"), the 2019 Spencer Stuart Board Index, and a New York City Comptroller's Boardroom Accountability Project report. All shared a common thread of calling for board refreshment to meet looming business challenges and that traditional views on board qualifications may need to be reconsidered.

In a 2016 Stanford Directors' College study, they found that the average director believes at least one director should be removed from their board as ineffective, more than a quarter believe directors do not give each other effective feedback, the structure for boards is not clear on removing directors who may no longer be qualified to serve based upon changing issues, and half

© Jennifer C. Wolfe 2020

J. C. Wolfe, *Disruption in the Boardroom*, https://doi.org/10.1007/978-1-4842-6159-0_7

believe that their board does not allow expression of honest opinions with only a few dominating discussion and decision making. Coupled with the annual NACD survey that shows only 56% of directors believe that the information they receive from management is sufficient to support informed decision making and oversight, it is clear that the time for change in the boardroom is now. The same study shows that boards are largely hearing primarily from their CEO, CFO, or General Counsel vs. subject matter experts in areas of information security, human resources, technology, risk, and strategy. Additionally, Delaware courts, which set the standard for corporate law, continue to shift their opinions on director risk oversight liability, which means directors could be exposed to more liability for risks from which they were previously sheltered.

According to a 2015 NACD annual survey, the top priorities of board members included

- Strategic planning and oversight
- Corporate performance and valuation
- Corporate growth/restructure
- CEO succession
- Executive talent management and leadership development

By the end of 2019, directors were most concerned about:

- Growing business model disruptions
- Slowing global economy
- Increased competition for talent
- Changing cybersecurity threats
- Accelerating speed of advances in technology

Consider for a moment how drastically the top issues changed in just a four-year span. After the 2020 Coronavirus Pandemic, health pandemics, new work environments, and uncertainty will be added to the list. The traditional five-year strategic plan on which boards typically rely for decision making is now obsolete when things change much faster than years ago.

All of the pressing issues outlined in this book are occurring when boards are already feeling maxed out on the amount of time they have available. In numerous surveys, directors express concerns that more engagement may not change their ability to oversee these areas. When many directors are also still serving in operating roles as a CEO, CFO, or senior executive of a large company of their own, it raises a legitimate concern about the amount of time directors must dedicate to their role and what is reasonable to expect of an individual.

In an age of disruption, the role of the board will change again in the next decade as it did in 2001 and 2008. It could come from best practices reshaping the board on its own process improvement initiative. It could come from public demands for greater accountability from corporations or pandemics that force change. It could come from government regulation. It could result from the 2020 Coronavirus Pandemic or future health crises. It is likely from all of the above.

Today, boards cite six major areas of governance: strategy, risk, cybersecurity, human capital, compliance, and Environmental Social Governance (ESG). And yet, most boards continue to rely upon the three-committee structure of audit, nominating/governance, and compensation. While many boards have already begun to create new committees related to technology, investment, compliance, strategy, research and development, corporate responsibility, or industry-specific needs, most have remained tethered by the primary three committees. Many directors I talk to express concerns that there simply aren't enough board members to have more than two or three committees. That is a fair argument. Outside of adding a significant number of new board members, it's not realistic that directors would serve on numerous committees and thus four is probably the maximum number of committees for the current board size, but there are differing opinions on that issue.

If you were to start from a blank page in today's climate, instead of band-aiding the legacy structure of boards, let's consider how we might define the role of the board. If our mission is to create a board of 8–12 people to provide oversight to a corporation facing today's challenges, what would be the core issues to be addressed by committees or subject matter expert groups?

- Financial accountability: Verify that the information the company reports out to investors and stakeholders is accurate. The board provides oversight on the overall financial health of the organization and provides counsel on what steps should be taken to ensure the financial stability of the company (i.e., including future capital investment needs). The board oversees that all SEC and other regulatory compliance requirements are met on a timely and accurate basis.

- Succession planning: The board carefully considers how the company will replace critical leadership roles in an orderly and thoughtful manner to avoid a crisis or absence of leadership. This would include the CEO, c-suite leadership, and fellow board members.

- Independence: The board ensures that the people in the room have the right skills and can make decisions independent of any personal financial or other gain tied to the company to truly look out for Stakeholder Values. They also keep the CEO in check to ensure there is not a rogue CEO acting in his or her own best interest vs. the stakeholders.

- Culture and incentives: The board monitors the organizational culture to ensure it incents people to engage in behavior that adapts to new technologies and disruptions and is respectful of all individuals. Directors ensure the compensation strategy for your key executives is properly aligned with all company goals and Stakeholder Values.

- Short and long-range strategy: The board ensures that the CEO and senior executives have developed a strategy for short-term needs that are essential to survival, but also with an eye on the future to "future proof" the business, to the extent that is possible. You assist with ensuring the budget is allocated to allow for innovative thinking about the future, and efficiently deliver operational effectiveness to be profitable in a responsible manner, including supply chain management and new technological developments.

- Security: Directors ensure there are clear checks and balances to provide the greatest possible security for employees, customers, and vendors (both cybersecurity and physical security). Directors engage independent thinking to trust but verify security measures are working and not overlooking obvious vulnerabilities.

- Governance and compliance: Directors ensure that the organization's structure and processes for providing this governance are in a state of continual improvement and constantly check for effectiveness. You ensure that all regulatory and compliance requirements are met, particularly regarding disclosures, providing checks and balances with the Audit Committee.

- Enterprise risk: The board defines the risks to the organization on a regular basis. What are the other issues that could harm the growth of the company including geopolitical, economic, sourcing and supply chain, environmental disasters, leadership failures? What is the company's risk appetite and ability to manage risk and balance investment against those risks?

- Mergers and acquisitions: Directors provide counsel on when and whether a merger or acquisition makes sense for the organizational goals. When it does, directors oversee culture and change management to derive the value of that acquisition.

- Environmental and social: Directors ensure that the company is acting responsibly as a good steward of the environment, the communities in which it serves, and is responsibly addressing issues of concern and the values of your stakeholders: shareholders, employees, customers, vendors, strategic partners, and the community in general.

- Crisis and business continuity: The board also prepares the organization for a crisis. Whether it is a cyberattack, an economic disruption, or a health crisis, the board has advisors and plans in place to protect stakeholders and respond with sage counsel and guidance.

That's a fairly tall order for a group of roughly ten people. It raises important questions. Does the size of the board need to change? Ten people is usually a good number to effectively function as a cohesive group. However, there may need to be additional advisors or subgroups that function to support the board as a whole. This is one of the issues that will need to be considered. Remember, boards started out primarily "rubber-stamping" management, which means a large board was not only not needed but detrimental. As generations shifted, the board became heavily responsible for financial transparency and ensuring there were not conflicts of interest, primarily to protect investors. This could also be done with a relatively small group. But today, we are asking a lot more of our boards. The question on size of the board is an important one.

Going back to our blank page in building a board environment, what would be the critical success factors for a board?

- The right people in the room: Whether you add board seats, refresh board seats, or simply hire board-focused advisors (i.e., they advise board members not the senior executives to avoid a conflict of interest), boards will need new skill sets and experience to ask questions and trust but verify what they are being told by management.

- Structure of committees, agenda, and board calendar: The very nature of board meetings may need to change structurally. When board members already feel maxed out, the agenda, committee structure, or approach may have to evolve. It needs to be designed for today's issues leveraging more remote capabilities, not tweaked from old structures and packing in more to in-person meetings.

- Prioritize what's most important for board decision making: This is obvious but is a complaint of many board members who cite they are fatigued with meetings and need to focus on what's most important. It may mean that more off-cycle meetings of smaller groups are needed to address emerging issues. It may also mean using remote meeting tools more effectively for "less important" matters. If the information is consolidated and presented in a more efficient manner, decisions could be made by board members without requiring the same amount of time in person, allowing in-person time for the most high-value functions.

- Present information effectively: This is also a big complaint of board members. Inundated with lengthy reports and PowerPoint presentations, it becomes overwhelming to prepare for a board meeting. Looking closely at process improvement in the boardroom in aggregating information most effectively is a critical part of the boardroom of the future.

Let's break each of these components of boardroom functions down to start to build a new matrix for the board and a fresh set of best practices.

The Right People in the Room: Board Refreshment and Composition

The average age of a corporate board member is 63.1. It is most common for directors to join a board in their 50s and 60s. Only 42% of boards now have a mandatory retirement at age 75. Of directors added, 37% are current CEOs of another company – that's more than one-third of board members out there currently serving as a CEO of their own company. A majority of new directors were previously a CEO or CFO, making top leadership and financial expertise still the most sought-after resume. This is understandable when you consider the history of boards and that the biggest reforms of the last 20 years dealt specifically with financial transparency and accounting.

But this is changing, and the need of the board to understand disruptive business models, new technologies, and a changing society and workforce along with cybersecurity means that same pattern may not work anymore. Only 2% of new board members had expertise in cybersecurity, 2% were entrepreneurial, and 3% were human capital or talent development experts. These are the three areas noted as top areas of concern for all boards as having the biggest impact on the boardroom of the future, and yet only 7% of board seats were filled with these skill sets.

This is completely out of synch with the changing needs and demands of the board. If everyone in the room has essentially the same resume, that doesn't really make sense, does it? You wouldn't build out your senior management team with all the same skill set. You would want different skills to address different matters. It begs the question, does the board need to reflect the subject expertise of the c-suite? For example, security, technology, and human resources may be needed to help create the culture of the future.

There are a couple of key questions to consider as you determine what the structure and composition of your board should be in the future. Getting the right people in the room doesn't have to mean the traditional way.

1. Should you have a director in each area of subject matter expertise needed to trust but verify what their counterpart in management is telling them (i.e., a checks and balances by function)?

2. Do you identify the skills matrix of each existing director and determine missing subject areas of expertise that may be needed? If so, do you consider filling board seats with new skill sets vs. the "prestige" factor of adding another CEO or CFO? This is often cited as a concern. "When the press release goes out, what will people say if we put an HR head instead of a CEO on the company board?" That fear is driving old-school decision making.

3. Could you alternatively hire independent experts in areas you are lacking to help your committees address new issues? For example, if the board itself hires a consultant or advisor to provide objective advice, that advisor would have a fiduciary duty to the board, not to the senior executives, to ensure there is no conflict of interest. If you've not worked in professional services, this is an important point. Whomever hires the professional and

pays them is who they answer to from a responsibility perspective. Many times, a senior executive may ask a consultant to a board to *not* to address certain issues; this is where the conflict comes in and why a board needs to have its own advisors separate from the operating company. The board may, in fact, need its own team of advisors in the future vs. relying upon the advisors already hired by the company executives.

■ **Note**   Is there a problem with using existing outside counsel, accountants, or consultants? Yes, there is. Any existing advisory relationships inherently have a conflict of interest. You need fresh, outside perspective that is not tied to advising or representing the senior executives of the company, but rather the board. Ideally, you should eliminate any other financial gain from the company than the board advisory role to ensure you receive objective advice. All too often, existing advisors are happy to "give away" or offer free education and advice to the board, but it comes with a price if they answer to management because it may not be fully objective.

---

4. Could you create a culture, cyber, or technology advisory board for the whole board to be available to answer questions in executive session, provide additional research, or help the board in assessing areas which might require additional expertise? This would allow you to have a paid advisory board separate from senior executives, but not formally part of the fiduciary board with a public presence.

5. Does your board adequately reflect your customer base so that you will hear the "voice of your customer" as you assess big decisions? I'm often shocked at how out of touch board members are with customers. What about your employee base? Who speaks for them or understands them? Who buys your products and why? Who is connected to that experience? A view into *Stakeholder Values* is critical in an age of disruption.

In light of the changing dynamics, a new skills matrix may be needed to evaluate if you have the right composition of your board and/or advisors with these skills. See Table 7-1. Check off if you have a director or a truly independent outside advisor with this skill on your board.

Table 7-1. Future Board Skills Matrix

Skill Set	Director with Skill	Independent Outside Advisor with Skill
Human capital and culture		
Sales and customer engagement		
Incentives and compensation; psychology		
Privacy, data compliance, and policy		
Oversight of artificial intelligence and understanding of unintended consequences of technology		
Cybersecurity and vulnerability		
Financial transparency and audit		
Financial strategy, credit, and analysis		
Enterprise risk management – business model disruption		
Supply chain management		
Strategic thinking and operational effectiveness		
Process improvement		
Governance		
SEC compliance		
Leadership and CEO		
Network infrastructure – technology		
Public relations and crisis management		
Innovation development		
Mergers and acquisitions and change management		
Environmental and social engagement with stakeholders		
Entrepreneurship and connection to incubators, cutting-edge business models		
Industry-specific policy and knowledge		

Structure of Committees and Traditional Board Agenda

There's no question that board agendas are already packed with the traditional functions and agenda items. In the past, most boards have been comprised of the following committees who meet as part of the board meeting process:

- Audit: The audit committee is required by the SEC as formalized in the 2002 Sarbanes–Oxley Act. It has three key roles and responsibilities: oversee the accuracy of financial reporting, ensure external auditor independence and review the company's system of internal controls, and ensure compliance with all laws and regulations. In recent years, the audit committee has become a catchall for other risk-related issues like cyber risk, enterprise risk, ESG, and corporate culture. This doesn't make sense in the context of the larger issues now facing boards. The audit committee is already tasked with one of the most important roles – financial accountability and transparency. The work in other areas should be spread to other or new committees.

- Nominating and Governance: The Nominating and Governance Committee is much like it sounds, responsible for shaping governance policies, preparing for board and committee succession, recruiting and onboarding new directors, driving board effectiveness through evaluations and education, and maintaining board charters, polices, and ethics.

- Compensation: The purpose of this committee traditionally has been to develop an executive compensation package that incentivizes the right behavior and moves the company toward its business goals. In this committee, outside experts or consultants have long played an important role in helping to guide decision making to be competitive. That same role may extend to these new areas.

Some companies also have a finance committee that functions to review the financial health of the company for budgeting and projections for various decisions that need to be made related to strategy and separate and apart from audit. Some have added a cyber or technology or risk committee to address related to those risks or committees related to industry areas.

Combining recommendations from NACD, the Society for Corporate Governance, Spencer Stuart, and Diligent, what follows is a fairly typical agenda and calendar.

Legacy – Traditional Board Agenda Sample

1. Opening Executive Session
   a. Vote – If needed on new board members or officers prior to starting a meeting
2. Call to Order
   a. Approval of minutes for most recent board meeting
3. Reports
   a. CEO
      i. Review of strategy approved by board
      ii. Suggested adjustment based on current developments
      iii. Special issues
   b. CFO Report
      i. Presentation of financial statements
      ii. Approval of financial statements
      iii. Review of budget adjustments
      iv. Review of current year financial projections
4. Report on company performance and operations – current quarter and year to date (delivered by senior management team)
   a. Board discussion of data presented
5. Report of Nominating and Governance
   a. Approval of minutes of most recent past committee meeting
   b. Confirmation of future board meeting dates
   c. Motion to elect new board member
   d. Action on resignation letter
   e. New risk committee charter approval
   f. Report on board evaluation

6. Report of Audit Committee

    a. Approval of minutes of most recent committee meeting

    b. Review of financial statements

    c. Review of financial projects

7. Report of the Compensation Committee

    a. Hiring and incentives

8. Decisions for the Board

9. Closing Executive Session

Legacy – Traditional Board Calendar

February	April	June
Board	**Audit Committee**	**Compensation Committee**
• 1-year assessment	• Internal and external audit reports	• Corporate incentive rating
• Dividend declaration	• Auditor appointment	• Executive incentive plan awards
• Growth strategy discussion	• Intangible asset review	• Deposit stock option grants
• Strategy review	• External auditor expense	• Approval of CEO individual objectives
	• Review financial aspects of business plan	• Proxy information
	• Financing update	• CEO performance appraisal
	• Long-term borrowing authorizations	**Nominating Committee**
	Board	• Corporate governance review
	• Authorization of foundation contribution	• New director candidates
	• Business plan review for next FY	**Board**
		• Business unit strategy review
		• Review of chairman's personal objectives
		• Dividend declaration
		• Annual meeting resolutions
		• Set calendar for next year

(continued)

September	October	December
Board	Strategic plan retreat for full board	**Audit Committee**
• Business unit strategy review		• Internal and external audit reports
• Annual organizational matters		• Risk assessment/compliance review
• Dividend declaration		• Officer and director expense review
• Annual shareholders meeting		• Senior financial and audit of personnel review
		Compensation Committee
		• Option grants
		Board
		• Management development updated
		• Dividend declaration
		• Strategy review

It's easy to see that most of this "traditional" board agenda and annual plan for boards focuses heavily on the financial health of the organization and traditional committee structures. To address these new and emerging issues, boards may need to consider adjusting or augmenting the traditional committee structure and taking a fresh look at the typical board meeting agenda along with the annual planning for when issues are addressed. A big part of this is to redefine these roles and redefine the skill set that may be needed to fill these committees.

A New Approach to Board Committees, Agendas, and Calendar

Again, boards would be wise to ask, if we were creating this as a new division of the company to provide oversight, how would we define it? If you determine that the right number of board members is 10–12, you really can't have more than four committees effectively. So, if four is the magic number, let's look at how we break down the new functionality required by committee.

- **Audit**. This function has been evolving since the 1970s when it was first introduced. The job is not getting any easier. For all companies, transparency in financial accounting, compliance with regulations, and ensuring that companies accurately represent the financial health of the company is critical to protecting investors, shareholders, and employees alike. Too much has been added to audit in the past as a "catchall" for risk. By adjusting the other committees, audit can remain focused on this critical function of boards to oversee the financial health of the organization. It makes sense for audit to be filled with directors who have expertise in finance in similarly sized organizations.

- Traditional roles of audit, as defined previously, plus:

  - Identify any potential conflicts of interest by senior executives or other board members with the business of the company.

  - Identify potential conflicts of interest by key advisors.

  - Evaluate the investment strategy of the company to meet short- and long-range financing needs.

  - The skill set needed for this committee will remain finance heavy where a former CEO or CFO is likely the right profile for this committee.

- Nominating and Governance: In addition to the traditional functions of nominating and governance such as recruiting new board members, recommending any change in governance practices, succession planning for the CEO, and other key executives, the role of this committee can evolve to fill certain gaps from the old approach. For example:

  - Conduct annual evaluations to determine if board members are fulfilling their duties and how the company as a whole is meeting its governance obligations. This should include a 360-peer review, which is frequently done under current best practices. It is also important to get feedback from senior executives, and in a new twist responding to environmental and social governance demands, consider interviewing other employees and potentially key vendors to know how the company is viewed from a responsibility perspective from more stakeholders.

  - Define stakeholders and their values for the rest of the board and seek out stakeholder opinions and data sets to present to the board. Develop a stakeholder engagement plan.

- Get feedback on the board structure, agendas, and committee effectiveness. Implement continuous improvement mechanisms, such as Six Sigma, to improve the efficiency of the board.

- Provide orientation to new board members to help them be successful.

- Evaluate what your CEO, senior executives, and fellow directors do and say publicly and on social media. This might include using software to track social media comments of the company and senior officers.

- Work with senior executives to streamline the processes and format of information presented to best meet the needs of the board members and committees.

- Good skills to have in these areas or resume features could benefit from nontraditional director roles or additional advisors to better meet the actual demands of performing this function.

  - Legal and compliance

  - Human resources and capital

  - Psychology

  - Process improvement

  - Research and analytics

  - Leadership

  - ESG

- Compensation and Culture: In addition to the traditional roles of setting compensation for the CEO and senior executives, this committee can begin to tackle the increasingly important role of culture in the organization, particularly as it relates to incentives. Consider the following areas of work for this committee:

  - Avoiding status quo thinking, checking for this in the organization

  - Innovation safe spaces to allow for disruptive thinking

  - Annual audit of culture

  - Whistleblower hotlines

  - Sales incentives throughout organization

- Day in the life of a customer/strategic partner
- Workplace hostility
- Environmental concerns of stakeholders and company footprint
- Social impacts
- Diversity
- Retention of talent
- Good skills for a director to have on this committee or in a specific advisor include
  - Human resources
  - Sales
  - Diversity and inclusion
  - Leadership
  - Psychology
  - Entrepreneurship
- Risk: A new risk committee can incorporate several of the other areas of potential exposure to the company. This can include the following:
  - Cyber risk and security
  - Business model disruption
  - New technologies and unintended consequences
  - Privacy and oversight of data
  - Crisis readiness
  - Outside audits of cybersecurity effectiveness
  - Enterprise risk management – adapting a framework for evaluating risks and developing a risk appetite for geopolitical, environmental, crisis, sourcing and supply chain, industry-specific threats
  - Good skill sets for this committee include
    - Cybersecurity
    - IT infrastructure and network security
    - Technology development
    - Innovators and disruptors

- Entrepreneurs from other industries
- Operating experience in disruptive areas
- Leaders outside of your industry who may see things from a different perspective
- Legal and compliance, risk managers

According to Spencer Stuart's 2019 US Board Index, among S&P 500 companies, risk committees are becoming somewhat more common than five years ago, with 12% of boards having risk committees, compared with 9% in 2014.

This four-committee structure is aligned with transitioning from legacy practices and board structure with adjustments to allow for these new disruptive areas in the boardroom to be more carefully considered. Much like audit relies upon outside auditors to provide advice, and compensation relies upon compensation experts, the other committees may also need outside reviewers, consultants, or audits to provide objective information and best practices to ensure that the company is addressing new and demerging areas. These are now equally important.

Broad groups of stakeholders will also likely continue to make ESG demands of management and director "thought leadership" in 2020 and immediately beyond. Developing new and robust ways of engaging all stakeholders is key to addressing growing expectations for corporate societal impact.

Committees may also more frequently convene by phone/web meeting and then report back at the larger board meetings of key whole-board areas for discussion to avoid over-meeting at the full board meeting. Agendas must also be reviewed for effectiveness. Consider ways to better leverage full board time and use more telephone or virtual meetings by committees and to carefully plan the time the full board is in session.

Refreshed Board Agenda with Disruption in Mind

1. Opening Executive Session

   a. Vote – If needed on new board members or officers prior to starting a meeting

   b. Refresh discussion of board assumptions on disruptive risks to the organization and agree upon questions to pose to CEO and senior management during the meeting regarding culture and responsibility to stakeholders. This is important to ensure board members are intellectually honest about questions they have for management before the meeting begins and hold each other accountable.

2. Call to Order

   a. Approval of minutes for most recent board meeting

3. Reports

   a. CEO

      i. Review of strategy approved by board

      ii. Suggested adjustment based on current developments and disruptive risks

      iii. Special issues

   b. CFO Report

      i. Presentation of financial statements

      ii. Approval of financial statements

      iii. Review of budget adjustments

      iv. Review of current year financial projections

4. Report of Risk Committee

   a. Status of outside cyber-readiness audit

   b. Crisis communication planning

   c. Other disruptive risks to consider (technology, business model shifts, societal shifts, health)

   d. Policy shifts that impact the organization

   e. Enterprise risk management framework review and status update

   f. Review of best practices on personal use of devices, technology

5. Report on company performance and operations – current quarter and year to date (delivered by senior management team remotely prior to the board meeting)

   a. Board discussion of data presented and additional questions

6. Report of Nominating and Governance

7. Approval of minutes of most recent past committee meeting

   a. Confirmation of future board meeting dates

   b. Motion to elect new board member

    c. Action on resignation letter

    d. New risk committee charter approval

    e. Report on board evaluation and continuous improvement planning for board effectiveness and ensuring all voices and viewpoints are heard

    f. Report on stakeholder values and assessment

8. Report of Audit Committee

    a. Approval of minutes of most recent committee meeting

    b. Review of financial statements

    c. Review of financial projections

    d. Financial health of the organization and future needs

9. Report of the Compensation and Culture Committee

    a. Status of independent reviews of culture

    b. ESG issues impacting stakeholders or concerns of developing problems

    c. Hiring and incentives

    d. Sales incentives throughout the organization

    e. Status quo culture, how is the organization allowing for change in response to changing dynamics

    f. Future human capital needs and development

10. Decisions for the Board

11. Closing Executive Session

    a. How are you trusting but verifying what management tells you? Discuss concerns about transparency or independent reviews that may be needed on issues of concern, particularly related to risk and culture.

    b. Hot topics discussion – select a topic for robust debate, invite a guest expert speaker for topic and ask that he/she provide both sides of any issue, then board has discussion, and conclude with new assumptions formed.

An important part of this revised schedule is to allow time to review assumptions the board has about disruptive risks and cultural issues in the organization, as well as to agree upon questions during executive session so that independent directors hold one another accountable and can express concerns about trusting but verifying what senior management is telling them.

It also closes with an executive session to regroup on those same trust issues, as well as carve out time for hot topics. You could also consider bringing in an outside expert to give you both sides of an issue to shake up your thinking and then engage in robust conversation. Always be sure to discuss what new assumptions you have after listening to a speaker. Did it change your thinking in any way?

An alternative annual calendar can also make time for more executive sessions of independent board members for discussions to occur by phone in preparation for board meetings. Committees may also want to tap into outside advisors to provide not just updates or briefings, but lead or facilitate conversations with the express purpose of helping the committee argue both sides of any issue to arrive at sound conclusions on the committee's beliefs and assumptions so that they can be documented and continually challenged and robustly debated. Understandably, it's hard to confront board members who shut down conversations, but outside advisors can help bear the brunt of that when needed. Without clearly defining your viewpoint as a board, it's difficult to maintain a sense of consistency.

This will generate more robust and intellectually honest thinking and lead to better outcomes. There's no more room for simply rubber-stamping what is presented, disruption requires real debate.

Additionally, boards should build in time to the annual calendar to visit R&D facilities or labs where innovative work is occurring. Directors should also seek out individual opportunities between board meetings to have a "customer" experience. Directors should also take time to shadow or visit with frontline salespeople and understand what challenges they are experiencing.

Disrupted Boardroom Best Practices Calendar Planning

Many of discussions related to technology, cybersecurity, ESG, or risk are often buried into committee work or lumped into a broader strategic planning. In the future, boards will need to integrate time for discussions and analyses throughout the year to continually "gut check" thinking when making decisions and ensure that disruptive forces are incorporated into traditional fiduciary and compliance duties of boards. Some of these functions are better performed or discussed in person, but many of these can be done by web-based meetings to limit travel costs and time for board members who are already maxed out. In the aftermath of the 2020 Coronavirus Pandemic, board members have grown more accustomed to using online platforms for meetings. This can allow more strategic planning of the calendar so that less is packed into the in-person meetings. What follows are events the Nominating and Governance

Committee should organize for the board in conjunction with committee chairs. Calendar planning by Nominating and Governance will become increasingly important. There is no one-size-fits-all calendar; industries and organizations may have differing driving forces. What follows can be carefully plotted on the annual calendar to meet your company's regulatory and industry-driven calendar.

- Digital mapping of disruptive risks: Once a year, develop assumptions the board has about disruptive risks to use as a base for making decisions throughout the year. Document this to use as a reference and hold one another accountable. Do this separate from strategic planning so you think independently of the plan the CEO is developing. This is most effective in person using a white board. This can be done as an "off-site" by the Risk committee and presented to the whole board. This exercise can benefit from an outside facilitator. This should be done annually and be led by the Risk Committee.

- Enterprise risk: An important annual exercise is to also formalize your risk appetite and full assessment of risks to the organization. There are many different models for enterprise risk. In this book, I've covered digital disruption, cybersecurity, societal shifts/the future of work, and environmental social. But there are other risks to consider: geopolitical, regulatory, competition, sourcing and supply chain, financial, health pandemics, and economic. The purpose of an enterprise risk approach is to annually update assumptions you have on what risks affect your business, what your appetite for those risks is (i.e., how much are you willing to spend to mitigate those risks), and your plan for responding to risks and continually monitoring them. This is another one that the Risk committee can tackle and present to the whole board. This should be done annually. It is also better in person using a white boarding session and led by the Risk Committee.

- 360 board evaluation (include perspective of stakeholders): Discussion of outcomes and continuous governance improvement. This can mostly be done remotely to reduce in-person time commitments. The use of an outside objective expert is essential to ensure the integrity of the process and that real feedback is given. See the following sample of the types of issues to address in a board evaluation. This should be done at least every other year. The facilitator may prefer to present the results in person, but if necessary due to travel limitations can be done effectively via online platforms. This effort can be led by the Nominating and Governance Committee.

- Management presentations via webinar: Subject matter experts within the organization prepare recorded webinars prior to board meetings to keep you updated without taking up time during board agendas that could better be used with discussion or questions. Current surveys show that the board hears primarily from the CEO and CFO, largely due to time constraints and the desire to control the narrative to the board. Consider giving other executives a chance to present to the board remotely using technology that allows for a one-hour presentation and discussion of the hot areas addressed in this book. This should be slated in between board members and allow boards to have access to different subject matter experts in the organization. This can be led by the Nominating and Governance Committee.

- Hot topic discussion: Engage experts to present both sides of hot issues and facilitate boardroom discussion to set new assumptions. This can be done remotely to allow for more education of board members. This does not need to take up time on an agenda or can be done over breakfast or lunch or even by phone and remote technology tools in between meetings. This should be done at least two to three times a year. This can be led by the Nominating and Governance Committee.

- Crisis readiness: Run a crisis readiness session on various topics – data breach, malware shuts down systems, #metoo moment of senior executive, environmental accident, life-threatening unintended consequence of your product, or, as we saw in 2020, a global health pandemic. This is most effective in person but could also be done remotely to test how you would react remotely in a real crisis. This should be done at least every other year and led by the Risk Committee.

- Culture assessment and discussion: An independent review of the health of the culture will help the board understand what's really happening. The assessment could be done internally with Human Resources or using an outside advisor to ensure objectivity. The presentation and discussion could be done by phone or in person, time permitting. This should be done at least every other year and every third year should be done by an outside objective party and led by the Compensation and Culture Committee.

- Talent pipeline and future of work discussions: Human Resources should lead a discussion among the board about how talent is being developed and how the organization is partnering with universities or high schools to find and curate talent and think about the workforce of the future. This can be done remotely and led by Human Resources and should be done annually and led by Compensation and Culture Committee.

- Competitive analytics: At least annually, have a thorough discussion of competitive intelligence. Your chief marketing officer or head of sales is most effective at delivering this information to you. All too often, the CEO likes to control or present information to the board, but this is really a disservice as access to subject matter experts helps boards. When it comes to understanding competition, ask the people who deal with it every day for your company. Also, consider running an analysis of the patents filed by your competitors as part of the exercise to know how you compare in innovation and new developments. This could also be done remotely to save time in person for high-value discussions and led by the Compensation and Culture Committee.

- Trust but verify: Discuss at least annually how you trust but verify what management tells you. How do you hold each other accountable? This should be done in person during executive session. This can be led by your lead directors.

Individual Board Member Activity During the Year

The following are actions individual board members should take every year. This does not have to be done as a whole board and, in fact, is often more effective if it is undertaken independently.

- Visit Research and Development Labs where innovative work occurs, ask questions to understand how they break the status quo culture, get budgets for new ideas, and find new ideas.

- Shadow or spend time with front-line salespeople to understand challenges they face in selling your product or service.

- Shop your company's product or service without alerting anyone that you are on the board. Actually, shop it as a customer would. This is critically important. Too many boards are given special treatment vs. a real customer experience; get the real experience. If you sell products online, compare the online experience to a competitor.

- Attend at least one continuing boardroom education conference (in person or virtually) or a conference on new technologies that impact your business.

- Visit production sites to understand how your product or service gets to market.

- Track social media of CEO and senior executives.

- Test whistleblower hotline. Does it work? What is the response?

Prioritizing What's Important

The board, as a whole, should continue to be responsible for oversight of the strategy of the organization ensuring that the CEO and executive team are prepared to execute on that strategy. Attention must be given to short-range and long-range thinking and risks that evolve. While the CEO and management team typically present and deliver the strategy, directors need to do some independent thinking to gut check themselves and ask tough questions. Whereas strategic planning used to be done every five years, that may need to change. While every year may be overly zealous for a board, some annual review or structured conversation about whether or not the assumptions on which the plans were based have changed would be appropriate given the pace of change.

An evolving best practice is for the risk and compensation/culture committee to take time once a year for their own planning and include a broad conversation about these big disruptive forces: digital/technological disruption, cybersecurity, and societal shifts (Figure 7-1). It is important for boards in a small group to take time to think about what is impacting your company, your customers, and your suppliers and form this as a set of shared assumptions to use when making decisions. A little bit of preparation can go a long way.

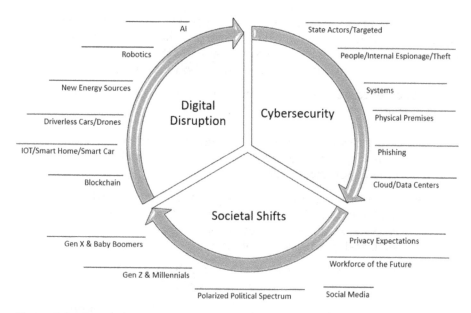

Figure 7-1. Digital Map

Digital Mapping Framework. A macro analysis framework of the shifts discussed in this book is provided as follows. I have referred to it as digital mapping. This means directors consider the impact of cybersecurity, digital disruption, and societal shifts on

- Your company
- Your suppliers
- Your competitors
- Your customers

An approach for committee members is to schedule about an hour per section and discuss how you think these facets of digital disruption, cybersecurity, and societal shifts will impact your company and how it will impact your suppliers, your competitors, and your customers. This will help you frame assumptions. If you map this out and document it, you have a good framework for making assumptions about the future that you can then use as a road map for making decisions throughout the year. You can do this yourself or consider bringing in subject experts in each of these areas to help guide your discussion and answer questions while you consider the impact on your stakeholders.

This should be updated annually with clear assumptions. If directors do this right the first time, it can serve as an important framework from which to make decisions about mergers and acquisitions, budgeting, investments, and risk assessment. The graphic of a digital map is just one example. It should be tailored to your specific industry and the areas of greatest impact to you. What follows is a broad overview that would impact most organizations. Write out your assumptions on these issues.

When it comes to disruptive risks identified in the mapping exercise, consider the following:

- Short-term growth opportunities: Do we have short-term opportunities for new sales, product, and services based upon these shifts?

- Long-term growth thinking: Are we effectively implementing "Labs" where innovative work can occur without an immediate return on investment? How are we tracking other forms of metrics?

- How are we partnering with universities or incubators to tap into longer-term trends and disruptors?

- Efficiency and operational effectiveness: Will any of these new shifts allow us to reduce time, money, and resources expended to increase profitability?

- Complete disruption: If we don't act fast enough, could we be completely disrupted?

It's not ever going to be the role of the board to completely set the strategy or execute on it, but to evaluate it, there needs to be some independent thinking about these issues. There have been questions posed at the end of each chapter that should also be considered. I have addressed in this book the new emerging areas of disruption, cybersecurity, societal shifts, and ESG. The fundamental questions related to supply chain, debt, long-term commitment, and crisis planning should also be considered.

Present Information Effectively

The final critical success factor for boards requires management to effectively present information and use time wisely. There are many complaints from board members that time is not spent most effectively, particularly when it comes to management presentations. Likewise, management is often concerned that they present information in a helpful way. This is where the role of the Nominating and Governance Committee can evolve to work with senior management to help streamline and improve the flow of information.

Senior management can also provide their "reports" in advance of board meetings through live or recorded webinars that allow board members to hear and review information and consider questions prior to the meeting rather than spending time in the board meeting with information gathering or presentations. The value of in-person time is in the engagement with one another to ask questions and weigh issues, not just sit all day and listen to information. This also allows more executives to be seen and heard with perspectives outside of just the CEO or CFO narrative. If presentations are given in advance, questions can be posed and potentially answered before the board meeting occurs, allowing more focused time for important discussion.

While certainly every company and industry may be different in their style and approach to information, directors can help by forming the questions they have and asking management to simply and concisely answer questions in less than 250 words with one slide per question. This can be done in advance of meetings to allow for focused discussion on the responses and eliminate redundancies.

Additionally, directors should ask management to always give both sides of any issue and cite objective resources for their opinions to avoid group think or biases.

If you find that you are not getting the information you need, consider creating a template for them to follow that better meets the needs of the board and consider filtering that outside of the in-person meeting. Presentation of information is, of course, important, but much of it can be done between meetings through more effective tools remotely.

Some rules of the road for management:

- Provide answers to pre-questions from board members in 250 words or less.

- Prioritize the information – what is the key takeaway – present that first, not data first.

- Prepare "webinars" or online presentations in advance of meetings that directors can live participate in to ask questions or watch again if needed.

- Present both sides of every issue when asking the board to make a decision or approve a decision.

- Make sure you hear from more than just the CEO, CFO, and General Counsel. Get subject matter experts deeper inside the organization to give more insights.

- Ask management to always incorporate thinking about disruption, cyber risk, cultural risk, and environmental or social risks associated with their strategy.

- Incorporate the voice of your customer into presentations.

- Consider bringing in designers or professionals at developing presentations to help you. You are a subject matter expert, not necessarily an expert presenter – get help if you need it.

Other Trends to Watch in the Boardroom

If the board does not self-evolve or disrupt, there may be other sources that demand it. Consider these final thoughts on what to watch for disruptive trends in the boardroom.

Mandated Changes – Legislation/SEC

The US Securities and Exchange Commission (SEC), the Public Company Accounting Oversight Board (PCAOB), and the Financial Accounting Standards Board (FASB) have put forward agendas for action in 2020, impacting financial reporting, accounting, auditing, and associated governance matters for companies. Boards should remain vigilant in their oversight role, staying informed of regulatory developments in a timely manner and understanding how their companies are monitoring and adjusting to regulatory changes.

The focus on cybersecurity is expected to continue to be based on:

- Moving from a mindset that focuses primarily on the prevention of cyber breaches to a more forward-looking perspective that also takes into consideration whether the companies are collecting data in such a way that the data can be protected

- Taking steps to ensure they are informing investors about material cybersecurity risks on a timely basis

- The importance of controls related to the identification and escalation of a cybersecurity incident to the appropriate levels within an organization

- The need to address cybersecurity incidents in insider-trading policies

- The nature of board involvement in the management of cyber risk

The pending Cybersecurity Disclosure Act would require boards to either have a dedicated board member with cybersecurity experience or explain why they don't have someone with such experience on the board. When companies know that it is not a matter of if, but when, it seems likely most boards will opt to add someone to the board. However, I question if that's entirely fair for a board to add someone with that expertise and then point a finger to that person as solely responsible for that entire broad area of risk. It's truly a whole-board responsibility. I've been in a boardroom where board members point to their Cybersecurity Information Officer and say, "that's what we have him for," in a joking manner. But all jokes aside, it was clear that's exactly what they did – they counted on one person to be responsible and shift the liability to him. That's not good governance.

The SEC is also working on the finalization of a proposed rule amending the reporting requirements of business disclosures, legal proceedings, and risk factors. This would add some of the issues addressed in this book as risk factors. While the timing and specific requirements of any final rule are uncertain, these proposals reflect the SEC's efforts to reassess current disclosure requirements. The SEC does remain concerned about short-termism by investors and companies focused on quarterly earnings over Stakeholder Values and held a roundtable on the subject.

It is also likely that some type of privacy legislation will come in the near future. As AI is deployed and more "accidents" or unintended consequence occur, expect to see more regulation on these areas as well. The SEC will continue to require greater disclosures and investigate failures by boards to address issues that cause public harm. Don't expect this to recede; expect much more of it in the future as the risks become greater and harder to control. In the aftermath of the 2020 Coronavirus Pandemic, it is likely we could begin to see health precautions as an area of risk for boards to address. How will your company ensure the health and safety of employees and customers alike? Everything addressed in this book has been highlighted in annual surveys by top governance experts. If action is not taken, expect the SEC to start reviewing and/or mandating it among public company boards.

Directors and Officers Liability and Insurance

The laws related to director liability have been changing, particularly in Delaware where so many companies are legally based. The Caremark case of 1996 set a very high bar for holding directors personally liable for failing to properly oversee their company's affairs. As boards refresh their oversight agendas in the years ahead, there are useful lessons to be drawn from decisions of the Delaware courts issued that allowed Caremark claims to proceed beyond the motion to dismiss stage (see Marchand v. Barnhill "Blue Bell"). Directors should identify their company's "mission critical" risks and ensure that information about these risks is elevated not only to management but also to the board itself.

Directors and officers of companies can be sued for a variety of reasons, including breach of fiduciary duty leading to financial losses, misrepresentation of company assets, misuse of funds, fraud, failure to comply with laws, theft of intellectual property, and lack of corporate governance, to name just a few. The climate toward corporations has been evolving to hold directors and officers more accountable, and insurers say risk is going up from years past.

According to Allianz, a global provider of insurance for boards, the five mega trends to watch include more "bad news" litigation, meaning litigation related to product problems, disasters, cyberattacks, and events other than just financial harm. They are also concerned about reputation damage and the failings of governance to oversee ESG issues. They also site an acceleration of securities class action suits and concerns about economic and political upheaval that will translate into claims against boards. "It's a tough time to be a director or officer of a company," said USI's national D&O practice leader, Andrew Doherty. He cited the changes to be related to the increased claims frequency and severity of claims, defense cost inflation and complexity, shareholder activism, and continuing M&A activity as reasons for the difficulties and increased cost to boards. He also states, "a well-thought-out strategy to proactively address issues and communicate effectively with carriers will go a long way in achieving the most optimal results."

Directors in the future will face greater personal risk and liability from holding their positions. It is imperative to fully understand the scope of what your D&O insurance will cover and what it will not. It also makes it clear that directors need to hold each other accountable. If you see a director who is not doing his or her part to address these issues of disruption and risk and to continue to learn and push thinking beyond existing assumptions, or, worse, stifling important discussions and alternative viewpoints, you may need to do something about it.

Additionally, the more you formally address and document the issues of risk and how you are considering them in the interest of your stakeholders, the better you demonstrate how you carefully exercised your duty of care.

Industry Best Practices

Finally, there are industry best practices formed by associations and groups that help shape the standards of good corporate governance. The National Association of Corporate Directors is the premiere association for good modern governance principles with significant resources available to members. Boards with full board membership also have access to boardroom speakers, education, evaluations, and support. The big consulting firms all provide annual surveys and reports.

The board should also consider continuous learning objectives – what areas are needed and how do you get objective sources of information. Send your directors to education programs like the ones at Stanford Directors' College, National Association of Corporate Directors Global Summit, and The Conference Board, to name just a few of the more prominent ones.

Look for provocative speakers to come in and shake up your thinking or perhaps present information in a new and different way. Look for dissonance and conflict instead of avoiding it or creating an echo chamber of what you already believe.

Embrace a culture of continuous improvement in your boardroom. High-performing boards assess the culture and dynamics in the boardroom to understand how they can operate more effectively. They use annual assessments to understand the performance and contributions of the board as a whole and those of the individual directors. See the following list of questions. These boards view composition as a strategic asset and take a formal approach to board refreshment, taking a multiyear view of departures and using assessments to strategically plan for board openings. To make the most of the increasingly diverse perspectives in the boardroom, boards should define and manage a board culture to facilitate constructive interactions between board members. For boards striving to be more dynamic, performance oriented, and shareholder focused, getting culture right is key.

Key Board Action Items to Be Ready for Disruption

- **New Skills Matrix for the Board**

Human capital and work culture
Environmental and social issues
Incentives and compensation – psychology
Privacy, data, and compliance
Oversight of artificial intelligence and understanding of unintended consequences
Cybersecurity and vulnerability
Financial transparency and audit
Financial strategy, credit, and analysis
Enterprise risk management – business model disruption
Supply chain management
Strategic thinking and operational effectiveness
Process improvement
Governance and oversight
SEC compliance
Leadership and CEO
Network infrastructure – technology
Public relations
Innovation development
Mergers and acquisitions
Industry-specific policy and knowledge

- **Board Composition**
  - How does your board match up to the skills matrix?
  - Do you need to refresh or add board seats?
  - Should you hire outside advisors to help fill the gap?
  - Are you on track to meet diversity quotas that are mandated by government laws or regulations or in demand from key stakeholders?
- **Committee Structure Reboot**
  - Audit: Streamline audit to focus on core competencies of financial transparency and regulatory compliance, as well as financial health of the organization.
  - Nominating and Governance: Implement continuous improvement and ensure the board is operating at best practices. Check the skills matrix of the board and engage outside help where needed.
  - Compensation and Culture: Audit the culture and consider the incentives in place to ensure that they match up to current risks and needs for adaptability in the organization. Work closely with Human Resources to consider how the workforce will shift with automation and be prepared.
  - Risk: Develop a risk committee to focus on implementing a framework and conducting annual assessments and assumption mapping for digital disruption, business model disruption, cybersecurity risk, enterprise risk, and workforce risks, and provide a "trust but verify" approach to work with management on risks.
- **Agenda Reboot**
  - Plan time before the board meeting for executive session to verify what questions you want to ask of management and hold each other accountable.
  - Refresh your assumptions about big disruptive risks to use as a guide in discussion with management.
  - Management presentations could be done in advance via web or recorded session to streamline time in session to robust conversation.

- Utilize more virtual off-cycle time for training, education, and innovative thinking.

- Evaluate the effectiveness of the board meeting agenda and be open to change to improve the use of time in person.

- **Events on the Board Calendar**

  - Schedule one time a year to assess risks associated with new technologies and disruptions, cyber risk, and societal shifts related to corporate culture.

    - Develop a clear risk appetite and set of assumptions to guide decision making.

    - Audit your culture at least once annually to understand the exposure you have from your own workforce.

    - Engage in future casting at least once a year – what are the big drivers that will impact everyone, as well as your industry?

    - Engage in a crisis simulation (i.e., cyber breach, #metoo moment with senior leaders, workforce backlash, geopolitical event, environmental event)

  - Create a road map for yourself.

    - Visit research and development labs and understand if you have a status quo culture.

    - Talk with frontline salespeople – understand the challenges they face in selling your products or services.

    - Identify educational events, either in person or online, to further your own personal growth as a board member.

    - Consider coaching on subject areas where you want support (i.e., technologies, disruption, etc.)

- **Board Evaluations – 360 Review and Process Improvement**

  - At least every other year, the board should conduct a 360 evaluation. Questions should be posed to individual board members about the board, as a whole, their role as an individual, and the leader director. The senior executive team should also be interviewed in the process. As defined in Chapter 6, an evolving trend is to also survey stakeholders for their viewpoint. Be sure to include customers, employees, and even strategic partners or vendors to understand how they view your company. Combined, this information can help the lead director and Chair of the Nominating and Governance Committee to implement continuous improvement.

- Sample Whole-Board Questions

    - Does the board include the right mix of expertise, skills, experience, and backgrounds?

    - Are directors given an equal opportunity to speak and provide input?

    - Are dissenting opinions allowed, encouraged?

    - Are alternate points of view or expertise sought out when making decisions?

    - Is there a balance between past performance and future trends that impact the business?

    - Do the reports and materials provide forward-looking business conditions, opportunities, risks, and emerging trends?

    - Is there a way for executives to elevate discussions to the board when needed?

    - Does the CEO allow other executives and subject matter experts time in front of the board?

    - Does the board receive sufficient information about industry, competitive, regulatory, customer, and other stakeholder developments including use of outside advisors?

    - Does the board engage its own advisors or rely up on advisors to the company executives?

    - Does the board give individual directors funding support for continuous education and improvement?

    - Does the board support individual directors in field visits (i.e., research and development, production, sales front line)?

- Does the board calendar include time for substantive discussion of risks and changes impacting the company? Including continually revisiting of assumptions on the strengths, weaknesses, opportunities, and strengths?

- Does the board allow for executives to change course when new information is presented without penalizing their incentives?

- Are leadership roles are based upon defined skills and leadership criteria?

- Do new board members match up to the right skill set not just a good press release?

- Sample Lead Director Questions

  - Does the lead director promote candid and rigorous discussion?

  - Ensure that all views are heard, including multiple or dissenting points of view?

  - Seek out positions of stakeholders?

  - Allow for constructive tension in board discussions?

  - Serve as a productive, efficient facilitator of conversation?

  - Lead executive sessions in a manner that allows you to trust but verify what you are being told? Allow for discussion of questions to ask of management?

  - Act as a champion of continuous improvement and avoid status quo culture?

- Sample Individual Director Questions

  - Is there a healthy respect for alternate opinions to your own?

  - Do you take a proactive approach to staying current on industry, competitive, customer, regulatory developments impacting the company including those addressed in this book?

  - Do you balance support of management with constructive challenges to trust but verify what you are told?

- Do you participate in ongoing director education?

- Do you withhold judgment when listening to others?

- Are you willing to take an unpopular position – moral courage?

- Do you understand emerging trends that could be disruptive?

- Are you properly prepared for board meetings?

- Do you hold other board members accountable?

- Do you take an intellectually honest position on bad news or reports of poor performance without punishing the messenger or executive presenting the information – seeks truth not blame?

- Are you receptive to feedback and calls for continuous improvement?

- Are you able to devote sufficient time to responsibilities?

- **General Principles**

  - Adopt an attitude of continuous improvement for yourself as a board member, your committee, and the board as whole – that is, be open to continuous change.

  - Pay attention to disruptive forces and be prepared for your industry to be upended.

  - Pay attention to cultural, environmental, and social issues.

  - Be prepared for a crisis.

Concluding Thoughts

We are entering a decade of profound change, kicked off with a global health pandemic that shut down the economies of the entire world. The consequences of new technologies and societal shifts along with increasing uncertainty are balanced with great benefits but also potentially devastating unintended consequences without the proper oversight. While oversight, itself, may emerge as a role among the c-suite, the board of directors will surely remain a trusted and needed source of good governance and oversight.

From tech startups with world-changing ideas to long-standing legacy companies, the new role of governance is to protect the interests of stakeholders – shareholders, employees, vendors and partners, customers, the community you impact. This means more than just financial transparency. It means we need individual directors and boards as a whole to act with

- *Intellectual Honesty*
    - Read and understand multiple points of view.
    - Trust but verify what management is telling you.
- *Moral Courage*
    - Question assumptions and have the courage to challenge old ideas and old incentive plans, and embrace the changes that are coming.
    - Don't allow a charismatic CEO to fool you.
- *Read, Learn, and Study*
    - Take the time to understand new technologies, cybersecurity, and societal shifts and do real homework.
    - If you don't continuously learn about new technologies, disruptive risks, cyber risks, and societal shifts, you really can't provide oversight effectively in a digital age.

The board of directors sets the cultural tone for the organization and holds senior management accountable for the decisions they make and actions they take. If the board of directors doesn't ask the CEO tough questions, who will? We now live in a time of continuous disruption. The future is changing rapidly, and if you only look to the past for guidance, you will miss the future. Business has always been about a continual preparation for the future requiring foresight. If you keep doing things the same way and fill the seats at the table with the same person, will your board be ready to respond to the next disruption?

Future Trends

How Do We Know What's Coming?

You may be asking, what's my source for all this information? How do I know what's coming and how do you make reasonable predictions about the future? There is no crystal ball, of course. We can only look to sources and signals to make reasonable predictions about the future. Here's how I approach thinking about the future and leveraging information available.

First, I aggregate and categorize daily news on the topics I have outlined here, as well as look for the emergence of new trends. I actually snapshot headlines and keep links in an electronic notebook as I track various trends. I always watch for bias and look for consistencies. When I find different reporters or sources report the same thing or find the same thing, I know we are on to a potential trend. I track on a regular basis: WSJ, Wired, Business Insider, TechCrunch, Harvard Business Review, and MIT Tech Journal. I also set up Google Alerts for key tech areas for outlier publications. I have all of my references listed by chapter in the back of the book.

Second, I track patents from a macro perspective of big technology companies. By looking at trends of what types of patents are being filed by big players such as Amazon, Google, Facebook, Intel, Apple, Verizon, AT&T, Netflix, and others, I gain an insight into what they are investing in protecting and what type of trends could emerge. I encourage senior executives to use patent analytics as a means of competitive intelligence and industry intelligence.

I also track financial analysts for any big moves by insiders. Bloomberg and Morningstar are good sources of information when trying to verify or confirm if a company is on the move with some new technology or if it's about to flop.

© Jennifer C. Wolfe 2020
J. C. Wolfe, *Disruption in the Boardroom*, https://doi.org/10.1007/978-1-4842-6159-0

Conferences and trade shows are also good ways to get a sense of what's going on and hear the hype. However, I caution that this is usually over hyped and you have to be thoughtful about what you hear, but it is important to aid in thinking outside the box. Dig deeper and raise questions about implementation but use this for inspiration and understanding: Consumer Electronic Shows, WSJ Future of Everything, South by Southwest, and Davos, to name just a few. There are many by industry and targeted to developers.

I look to reports from Futurist Societies and Organizations. All of these have a bias (political or financial), so look for that and understand or recognize it to interpret the trends accurately. I watch for consistencies across the organizations. I follow Insights Association, MIT Labs, The Futures Institute, The Future Today Institute, Institute for the Future, World Future Society, and the Association of Professional Futurists, among others.

Finally, I recognize that with all of the new information and new technologies, most of these transformations have occurred before with earlier technologies. For example, I study how the IBM SQL database changed the industry. I look at how HTML code changed websites and created the digital age. I look at how Bluetooth emerged as the consolidated standard form of wireless technology. I look at when Oracle made Java open source code (i.e., free and open to use and scale), and it changed everything. It ushered in the era where companies like Google and Facebook welcome outside engineers to use their code and build up on it. There are so many examples from just the last few decades in how society changed and morphed and all of it repeats itself in different forms.

Fundamental Technology in Today's Key Trends

Trend	What It Is	Components	How It's Used	Benefits	Challenges	Top Trends and Future Opportunities
Artificial Intelligence (AI)	• The use of computer code and algorithms combined with data inputs to simulate human intelligence and power devices or robots. • Provides solutions to problems where data sets or complexity is too great. • Continuously learning based upon inputs, algorithms, and interactions with data.	• Explosion of data to draw from • Smart algorithms are improving to provide for deep machine learning • Computing resources in the cloud and greater infrastructure • See objectives in text, pictures, video • Hear and capture spoken commands • Communicate using natural language • Sense biometrics or physical inputs • Think and apply learning	• Data assembly and analytics • Sales order management, price monitoring, self-serving • Automating operations	• Cost savings • Optimized analytics and use of data continuously • Faster ROI than humans • Improved productivity and quality • Free up management workers for higher-value tasks	• Trust in the AI • Training employees to oversee and work within AI • Legacy systems • Disruption to existing • Governance and security to overcome bias • Cyber risks and scale	• Retail • Automotive • Energy • Telecommunications • Health care • Financial Institutions • Manufacturing

(continued)

Trend	What It Is	Components	How It's Used	Benefits	Challenges	Top Trends and Future Opportunities
Robotics	• Devices and robots that mimic the role of humans faster and less prone to error. • Primarily used for strictly rule-based repetitive processes. • Requires AI and programming to work.	• Hardware: the robot • Networks: how it connects – getting faster • Interface – with other devices and your user interface • Security protocols to authenticate and encrypt data and protect against hacking	• Data assembly and analytics • Sales order management, price monitoring, self-serving • Automating operations	• Cost savings • Optimized analytics and use of data continuously • Faster ROI than humans • Improved productivity and quality • Free up management workers for higher-value tasks	• Oversight that robots perform as intended – no unintended consequences • Workforce evolution and change management	• Construction • Drones/military
Internet of Things ("IoT")	• Things you touch in your life connected through the Internet or other computer networks. • Car, bed, refrigerator, wearables, clothing, mirrors, toilets, biometric sensors, machinery, doors, doorbells, etc.	• Hardware: the things • Networks: how it connects • Interface: with other devices and your user interface • Security protocols to authenticate and encrypt data	• Smart Everything (agriculture, health care, cities, financial services, manufacturing)	• Enrich experiences with data • Long-term cost savings • Standardize and integrate with AI, robotics, and blockchain	• Privacy and security • Disruption to traditional jobs and work • Scalability	• Monetization of data collected • Integration with blockchain, AI • Evolution away from traditional cloud to blockchain or other ways of connecting • 5G will increase capabilities • Security for IOT will rapidly expand

References

Chapter 1

Ackerman, Jason, The Future of supermarkets, The Wall Street Journal, April 26, 2015.

Ajaz Ahmed and Stefan Olander, Velocity: The Seven New Laws for a World Gone Digital. Vermilion, 2012.

Allam, Chantal, WeWork scrambles to remove office phone booths after cancer causing agent found, WRAL TechWire, October 25, 2019.

Andriotis, Annamaria, Equifax board members re-elected despite massive data breach, Wall Street Journal, May 4, 2018.

Arbesman, Sam and Dane Stangler. What Does Fortune 500 Turnover Mean? The Ewing Marion Kauffman Foundation, 2012.

Arends, Brett, Equifax hired a music major as chief security officer and she has just retired, MarketWatch, September 15, 2017.

Arnold, Chris, Equifax CEO Richard Smith Resigns After Backlash Over Massive Data Breach, NPR, September 26, 2017.

Atkinson, Robert D. & Ezell, Stephen J. "Innovation Economics: The Race for Global Advantage" Yale University Press, 2012.

Associated Press, Tesla and other electric car batteries lose 40% of their range in extremely cold weather, AAA tested the BMWie3, Chevrolet Bolt, Nissan Leaf, Tesla Model S75D and Volkswagen e-Golf, Market Watch, February 7, 2019.

J. C. Wolfe, *Disruption in the Boardroom*, https://doi.org/10.1007/978-1-4842-6159-0

Ballmer, Steve on Fox Business News https://video.foxbusiness.com/v/6103922677001/#sp=show-clips.

Balu, Nivedita, Johnson, Eric, Boeing board strips CEO of chairman title amid 737 Max crisis, Reuters, October 11, 2019.

Basak, Sonali, JP Morgan's We work IPO pursuit was many years and loans in the making, Bloomberg, August 6, 2019.

Bellis, Mary, "Putting Microsoft on The Map." About.com, March 15, 2012.

Bensinger, Greg. "Rebuilding History's Biggest Dot-Com Bust," The Wall Street Journal, January 12, 2015.

Benoit, David, Farrell, Maureen, Brown, Eliot, WeWork is a mess for JP Morgan. Jamie Dimon is cleaning It up, Wall Street Journal, September 24, 2019.

Bogost, Ian, Artificial Intelligence Has Become Meaningless, The Atlantic, March 4, 2017.

Brayer, Elizabeth, George Eastman: A Biography, Baltimore: Johns Hopkins University, 1996.

Captain, Sean, We Work's laughably weak Wi Fi password is downright dangerous, Fast Company, August 21, 2019.

Carreyrou, John, Bad Blood, Secrets and Lies in a Silicon Valley Startup, New York: Knopf, 2018.

Carreyrou, John, Theranos Whistleblower Shook the Company and His Family, WSJ, November 18, 2016.

Coyne, Kevin, Patricia Clifford, and Renée Dye, Breakthrough Thinking from Inside the Box, Harvard Business Review. 2007.

The Inventor: Out for Blood in Silicon Valley, HBO 2019, Produced by Alex Gibney, Jessie Deeter and Erin Edeiken.

Carlson, W. Bernard, Innovation as a Social Process: Elihu Thomson and the Rise of General Electric, 1870-1900, New York: Cambridge University, 1991.

Chesbrough, Henry, Open Business Models: How to Thrive in the New Innovation Landscape. Boston: Harvard Business School, 2006.

Chiu, Jeff, Theranos CEO Elizabeth Holmes' criminal fraud trial is set for July 2020, Associated Press, June 29, 2019.

Chunka Mui, How Kodak Failed Forbes, January 18, 2012.

Collins, Jim. Good to Great: Why Some Companies Make the Leap...and Others Don't, New York: Harper Business, 2001.

Collins, Jim and Jerry Porras. Built to Last: Successful Habits of Visionary Companies. New York: Harper Collins, 1997.

Collins, Douglas. The Story of Kodak. New York: Abrams, 1990.

De Lea, Brittany, Theranos' Elizabeth Holmes in California court ahead of trail date, Fox Business January 14, 2019.

Drucker, Peter, The Essential Drucker: The Best of Sixty Years of Peter Drucker's Essential Writings on Management (Collins Business Essentials) Paperback – July 22, 2008.

Drucker, Peter, Management: Tasks, Responsibilities, Practices. New York: Harper & Row, 1974.

"Eastman Kodak Company," www.fundinguniverse.com/company-histories/Eastman-Kodak-Company-Company-History.html.

"Eastman Kodak Co. (EK): Profile," http://finance.yahoo.com/q/pr?s=ek (last accessed October 15, 2009).

"Evolution of our brand logo." www.kodak.com/global/en/corp/historyOfKodak/evolutionBrandLogo.jhtml (last accessed October 15, 2009).

Eliot, Lance, Boeing 737 Max 8 and Lessons for AI: The case of AI self-driving cars, AI Trends, March 22, 2019.

Elliot, Megan, 17 Great companies that came back from the brink of death, Showbiz CheatSheet, December 13, 2018.

Fadell, Tony, All Around Us, Nothing but Net, The Wall Street Journal, April 26, 2015.

Fahden, Allen. Innovation on Demand: How to benefit from the coming deluge of change: make creativity work for you and your company. Minneapolis: The Illerati, 1993.

Farrell, Maureen, and Brown, Eliot, The money men who enabled Adam Neumann and the We Work Debacle, Wall Street Journal, December 14, 2019.

Feuer, William, Airbnb suffers setback in Jersey City as residents vote to regulate short-term rentals, November 5, 2019, CNBC.

Friedman, Thomas, The World is Flat: A Brief History of the Twenty-First Century. New York: Farrar, Straus and Giroux, 2005.

Freund, Alexander, Boeing crash: Can machines make better decisions than people? DW.com, March 15, 2019.

Fussell, Sidney, Airbnb has a hidden camera problem, The Atlantic, March 26, 2019.

Gertner, Jon, The Idea Factory: Bell Labs and the Great Age of American Innovation, Penguin Books: February 26, 2013.

Gertner, Jon, Like Building Refrigerators: Bell Labs and The End of Game-Changing Innovation, Time, March 27, 2012.

Gevurtz, Franklin, The Historical and Political Origins of the Corporate Board of Directors, Hofstra Law Review, Volume 33 Issue 1, 2004.

Green, Scott, A look at the cause, impact and future of the Sarbanes-Oxley Act, The Journal of International Business Law, Volume 3, Issue 1, Article 2.

Green, Dennis, Target's CEO reveals how he fixed a mistake that was costing the company customers, Business Insider, July 18, 2017.

Gordon, John Steele, What digital camera makers can learn from George Eastman, American Heritage, October 2003.

GQ Staff, The Tale of How Blockbuster Turned Down an Offer to Buy Netflix for Just $50M, GQ, September 19, 2019.

Hazleton, Lesley, Jeff Bezos: How He Built a Billion Dollar Net Worth Before His Company Even Turned A Profit, Success, July 1998,

Hafner, Katie, Where Wizards Stay Up Late: The Origins of The Internet First, Simon & Schuster, 1996.

Heppelmann, James and Michael Porter. How Smart, Connected Products Are Transforming Competition, Harvard Business Review, October, 2015.

Holmes, Alan, The 13 Biggest Tech company Failures in the Last 10 Years, Business Insider, December 24, 2019.

Hongkiat, What Happens in an Internet Minute, www.hongkiat.com/blog/what-happens-in-an-internet-minute-infographic/ October 20, 2015.

Holman, W. and Jenkins, Jr., Google and the Self-Driving Delusion, The Wall Street Journal, January 6, 2015.

Huntsman, Jon, Trade Gets More Important- and Complex, The Wall Street Journal, April 26, 2015.

How Amazon Cleared the Profitability Hurdle, Business Week, February 4, 2002.

Jeffrey, Don, Amazon.com Eyes Retailing Music Online, Billboard, January 31, 1998, pp. 8-9.

Johnson, Eric, General Magic tried to invent a smartphone in the 1990s. This is why it failed. Recode, July 30, 2018.

Johnson, Steven, How We Got to Now: Six Innovations That Made the Modern World, Riverhead Books, 2014.

Kaplan, Philip J. F'd Companies: Spectacular Dot.com Flameouts. New York: Simon & Schuster, 2002.

Kakad, Sangram, From Bankruptcy to a Trillion Dollar valuation: An untold story of Apple, Meidum.com, August 4, 2018.

Khan, Mehreen, Ram, Aliya, Uber faces tougher regulation after ECJ rules it is a transport service, December 20,2017, Financial Times.

"Kodak: About Kodak: History of Kodak," www.kodak.com/global/en/corp/historyOfKodak/historyIntro.jhtml (last accessed October 15, 2009).

Keenan, Alexis, Boeing board members need to step down: 737 ax crash victim's father, Yahoo News, December 23, 2019.

KnowledgeWorks Foundation. 2020 Forecast: Creating the Future of Learning. Creative Commons License Attribution Share Alike, KnowledgeWorks Foundation and Institute for the Future, 2008.

Khosla, Sanjay and Mohanbir Sawhney, Where to Look for Insight, Harvard Business Review, November, 2014.

Koller, Daphne. Exit the Sage on the Stage, The Wall Street Journal, May 13, 2015.

Kraus, Rachel, Aggressive and riskier AI – and bureaucracy – caused the Boeing crashes, report says, Mashable, June 2, 2019.

Lane, Ben, Wells Fargo board shakeup continues: longest serving directors set to retire, March 2, 2018, Housing Wire.

Lafley, A.G. and Ram Charan. The Game-Changer: How You Can Drive Revenue and Profit Growth with Innovation. New York: Crown Business, 2008.

Lash, Herbert, In new headache, WeWork says it found cancer-causing chemical in its phone booths, Reuters, October 14, 2019.

Leiva, Ludmila, Here are the Theranos Investors Who Lost Millions, Refinery 29, March 5, 2019.

Leiva, Ludmila, Here are all of the Elizabeth Holmes Criminal Charges, March 11, 2019.

Levitt, Hannah, Hamilton, Jesse, Wells Fargo Regulator Punishes Leaders who spun Culture of Fear, Bloomberg, January 23, 2020.

Levitt, Steven D. & Dubner, Steven J. Super Freakonomics: Global Cooling, Patriotic Prostitutes and Why Suicide Bombers Should Buy Life Insurance." HarperCollins 2009.

Isaacson, Walter, The Innovators: How a Group of Hackers, Geniuses, and Geeks Created the Digital Revolution Simon & Schuster, October 6, 2015.

Kulwin, Noach, Theranos CEO Elizabeth Holmes's Five Best cover store Appearances, Ranks, Vox, October 26, 2015.

Mason, John, Boeings Culture: The Board of Directors Included, Seeking Alpha, January 14, 2020.

McBride, Sarah, Tan, Gillian, Turner Giles, Elstron, Peter, Alpeyev, Pavel, and Stone, Brad, The Prodigal Son, Bloomberg Business Week, December 23, 2019.

McEnery, Thornton, Adam Neumann's Active Fantasy Life Includes an Intimate Future Relationship with Jamie Dimon, Deal Breaker, September 24, 2019.

McKenna, Francine, Founder Holmes raised $700 million from investors but never hired accountants to produce audited financial information, MarketWatch, March 20, 2018.

Moritz, Scott, Verizon Admits Defeat with $4.6 billion AOL-Yahoo Write Down, Bloomberg, December 11, 2018.

Overly, Steven, Uber Hires Eric Holder to investigate sexual harassment claims, The Washington Post, February 21, 2017.

Palmer, Annie, We Work CEO returns $5.9 million the company paid him for 'We' trademark, CNBC, September 4, 2019.

Palmer, Annie, Travis Kalanick severs all ties with Uber, departing board and selling all his shares, CNBC, December 24, 2019.

ParisTech Review and Knowledge@Wharton. 2020 Foresight: Predictions for the next Decade. ParisTech Review, 2011.

Pletz, John, Outcome Health founders indicted in fraud scheme, Crain's Chicago Business, November 25, 2019.

Popken, Ben, Equifax execs resign security head, Mauldin, was Music Major, NBC News, September 15, 2017.

Porter, Michael, Competitive Strategy: Techniques for Analyzing Industries and Competitors, Simon & Schuster, 1985.

Porter, Michael. Competitive Strategy: Techniques for Analyzing Industries and Competitors. New York: The Free Press, 1980.

Primack, Dan, Was Uber smart to hire Eric Holder, Axios, June 20, 2017.

Pagones, Stephanie, Ex Theranos CEO Elizabeth Holmes providing own defense in civil suit: Fox Business January 25, 2020.

Price, Nicholas, What is the history of corporate governance and how has it changed? Diligent Insights, October 3, 2018 .

Ramsey, Lydia, how Elizabeth Holmes convinced powerful men like Henry Kissinger, James Mattis and George Shultz to sit on the board of now disgraced blood testing startup Theranos, Business Insider, March 19, 2019.

Rapp, David "Inventing Yahoo!." American Heritage, www.americanheritage. com/events/articles/web/20060412-yahoo-internet-search-engine-jerry-yang-david-filo-america-online-google-ipo-email. shtml, 2006.

Rekdal, Andreas, Outcome Health headquarters, plans to add 2,000 jobs, Built In CHI, September 26, 2017.

Richter, Felix. E-Commerce in the United States, Statista. 2012.

Rigby, Darrell, Digital-Physical Markups, Harvard Business Review, September, 2014.

Rocha, Euan. BlackBerry CEO sees fewer new devices, focus on profitability, Reuters, November 9, 2014.

Satariano, Adam, Google Fines $1.7 billion by EU for Unfair Advertising rules, New York Times, March 20, 2019.

Schafer, Lee, Three years on, the Wells Fargo scandal is still breathtaking, Star Tribune, January 25, 2020.

Schechner, Sam, Facebook faces potential $1.63 billion fine in Europe over data breach, Wall Street journal, September 30, 2018.

Schulze, Elizabeth, If you want to know what a US tech crackdown may look like, check out what Europe did, CNBC, June 7, 2019.

Schmidt, Eric & Cohen, Jared. The New Digital Age: Reshaping the Future of People, Nations and Business, Alfred A. Knopf, 2013.

Seidel, Jamie, How a Confused AI may have fought pilots attempting to save Boeing 737 Max's, News Corp Australia, March 19, 2019.

Sheetz, Michael, Secretary DeVos, Walmart heirs and other investors lost over $600 million on Theranos, CNBC, May 4, 2019.

Son, Hugh, Jamie Dimon says WeWork will survive and that he's learned some tough lessons from the debacle, CNBC, November 5, 2019.

Stadler, Christian, The Four Principles of Enduring success, Harvard Business Review, July 2007.

Silver, Nate, The Signal and the Noise: Why so Many Predictions Fail — but Some Don't, Penguin Press, 2012.

Sinek, Simon, Start with Why, Penguin, 2009.

Strauss, Daniel, JPO Morgan CEO Jamie Dimon says we work's IPO debacle taught him a few key lessons, Markets Insider, November 5, 2019.

"The History of Yahoo!- How it All Started," http://docs.yahoo.com/ info/misc/history.html, 2005.

Tynan, Dan, The Glory that was Yahoo, Fast Company, March 21, 2018.

Thangavaelu, Poonkulai, Companies that went bankrupt from innovation lag, Investopedia, October 15, 2018.

Thomas, Lauren, Sears, Mattress Firm and more: Here are the retailers that went bankrupt in 2018, CNBC, December 31, 2018.

Thompson, Amy, Lanxon, Nate, Uber's London license ban marks global regulatory backlash for ride-hailing firms, Insurance Journal, November 27, 2019.

Tregoe, Benjamin and John Zimmerman. Top Management Strategy: What it is and How to Make it Work, New York: Simon & Schuster, 1980.

United States of America Department of The Treasury Complaint Against Former Wells Fargo Executives www.occ.gov/static/enforcement-actions/eaN20-001.pdf.

Whittaker, Zack, Equifax breach was entirely preventable had it used basic security measures, says House report, TechCrunch, December 10, 2018.

Willings, Adrian, 34 tech brands that spectacularly went bust or disappeared from existence, Pocket-lint, December 18, 2019.

"Yahoo! Inc.," www.fundinguniverse.com/company-histories/Yahoo-Inc-Company-History.html.

"Yahoo! Inc. (YHOO): Profile," http://finance.yahoo.com/q/pr?s=YHOO (last accessed October 15, 2009).

Chapter 2

Brownfield, Andy, Here's What Macy's CEO Lundgren had to say about competing with Amazon, Cincinnati Business Courier, March 22, 2016.

Carool, Paul and Mui, Chunka, Billion Dollar Lessons, Penguin Group 2008, 2009.

Greene, Ryan, CEO Doug McMillon Discusses Innovation and the Future of Walmart, Action IQ, March 2017.

Haddon, Heather, America's Biggest Supermarket company Struggles with Online Grocery Upheaval, Wall Street Journal, April 21, 2019.

Ignatius, Adi, We Need People to Lean into the Future, Harvard Business Review, March – April 2017.

Janis, Irvin, Groupthink, University of Notre Dame Press, 1971.

Nassim Nicholas, Taleb, Fooled by Randomness, the Hidden Role of Chance in Life and in the Markets, New York Random House, 2004.

Taleb, Nassim, The Black Swan, The impact of the Highly Improbable (New York Random House, 2007.

Wladawsky-Berger, Irving, Innovation and National Security in the 21st Century, Wall Street Journal, January 17, 2020.

Chapter 3

Ackerman, Evan, The Electronic Highway: How 1960s visionaries presaged todays' autonomous vehicle, IEEE spectrum, August 2, 2016.

Balasubramanian, Manikandan and Pramath Malik, In search of the next patent war, Intellectual Asset Management Magazine, June 1, 2015.

Banker, Steve, Will the autonomous truck race require greater simplicity, Forbes, September 1, 2019.

Batra, Neal, Betts, David, Davis, Steve, Force of change the Future of Health, Deloitte Insights, April 30, 2019.

Berman, Dennis and Jerry Wolfe, Big data's Promise, Peril, The Wall Street Journal, October 5, 2015.

Bhuiyan, Johana and Charlie Warzel, God View: Uber Investigates Its Top New York Executive For Privacy Violations, BuzzFeed, November 18, 2014.

Bloomberg Business Week, the Year Ahead Special Issue, October 28, 2019.

Boorstin, Julia, Era of mega-funded, money losing unicorn startups is coming to an end, CNBC, January 23, 2020.

Borland, Kelsi Maree, Do we have the infrastructure for driverless cars? Globe Street.com, December 13, 2018.

Brown, Brad et al. Big data: The next frontier for innovation, competition and productivity, McKinsey & Company, 2011.

Buchholz, Scott, Briggs, Bill, Deloitte Tech Trends 2020.

Burgess, Matt, Wired explains What is the Internet of Things, Wired UK, February 16, 2018.

Calder, Simon, Gatwick airport drone shutdown could have been an inside job, Independent, September 27, 2019.

Carrier, Ryan, Implementing Guidelines for Governance, Oversight of AI and Automation, Communications of the ACM, February 12, 2019.

CB insights, 38 Ways drones will impact society: from fighting war to forecasting weather, UAVs change everything, Research Briefs, January 9, 2020.

Clifton, Brian, Successful Analytics: Gain Business Insights by Managing Google Analytics, Advanced Web Metrics, 2015.

Chapin, Lyman, Scott Eldridge, and Karen Rose, The Internet of Things: An Overview, The Internet Society, 2015.

Cheng, Roger, The 5G wireless revolution, explained, CNet, October 27, 2019.

Chin, Josh, The Internet Divided Between the US and China, Has Become a Battleground, Wall Street Journal, February 9, 2019.

Christian, Anderson, What to expect from virtual reality in the future? Thrive Global, November 19, 2019.

CMO C-Suite Studies, From Stretched to Strengthened: Insights from the Global Chief Marketing Officer Study, IBM Corporation, 2011.

CNN Library, Enron Fast Facts, Last Updated April 24, 2019.

Columbus, Louis, The Best Big Data and Business Analytics Companies to Work for In 2015, Forbes, May 9, 2015.

Cook, Tim, Tim Cook: TV, Cars, Watches and More, The Wall Street Journal, October 27, 2015.

Copeland, B.J. Artificial Intelligence, Encyclopedia Britannica,

Daniel, Tony, Makes the Case for Trust Busting Big Tech Companies, The Federalist, June 14, 2014.

Dastin, Jeffrey, Amazon scraps secret AI recruiting tool that showed bias again women, Reuters, October 9, 2018.

Davis, Bob and FitzGerald, Drew, 5 G Future Ready, Wall Street Journal, February 4, 2020.

Delooper, Christian, What is 5? Digital Trends, November 18, 2019.

D'Onfro, Jillian, AI 50: America's most promising artificial intelligence companies, Forbes, September 17, 2019.

Dull, Tamara, A Non-Geek's Big Data Playbook, SAS Best Practices.

Dredge, Stuart, 91% of top brands have apps, but how many of them are any good?, The Guardian. October 28, 2011.

Duvall, Tyler, Hannon, Eric, Katseff, Jared, Safran, Ben and Wallace, Tyler, A New look at autonomous vehicle infrastructure, McKinsey & Company Resources, May, 2019.

Dwoskin, Elizabeth and Deepa Seetharaman, Facebook Restricts Access to Its Data Trove, The Wall Street Journal, September 21, 2015.

The Economist, White Paper by Toray, The future of healthcare, The Economist, 2017.

Finley, Klint, The Wired Guide to Net Neutrality, Wired, May 9, 2018.

Forbes Technology Council, 15 unexpected consequences of GDPR, Forbes, August 15, 2018.

Forester, Jim, Weather creates challenges for next generation of vehicles, Forbes, November 22, 2019.

Fraser, Ian, Five predictions for the future of money, Raconteur, March 15, 2019.

Goldman, Jake and Ben Ilfeld, iOS 9 Content Blockers: Impact Analysis and Mitigating Strategies, 10up. September 23, 2015.

Garber, Jonathan, Housing market come back heats up, Fox Business News, November 27, 2019.

Gottfried, Miriam, How Cable Companies Can Capture the Mobile Internet, The Wall Street Journal, September 22, 2015.

Google Seeks Richer Role With Own Content, The Wall Street Journal, February 7, 2014.

Gorman, Megan, How millennials are revolutionizing the home buying process, Forbes, August 31, 2019.

Graziano, Kent, The true impact of GDPR is emerging now, CIO Dive, May 20, 2019.

Guimarães, Thiago, Revealed: A Breakdown of the Demographics for Each of the Different Social Networks, Business Insider, January 23, 2015.

Hao, Karen, This is how AI bias really happens – and why it's so hard to fix, MIT Technology Review, February 4, 2019.

Harder, Amy, Bill Gates faces daunting nuclear energy future, Axios, July 15, 2019.

Hazlett, Thomas, The New Trustbusters Are coming for Big Tech, Reason, October, 2019.

Hendler, James, As governments adopt artificial intelligence, there's little oversight and lots of danger, Phys.org, April 18, 2019.

Heppelmann, James and Michael Porter, "How Smart, Connected Products are Transforming Competition, Harvard Business Review, November, 2014.

Hennigan, W.J., Experts say drones pose a national security threat and we aren't ready, Time, May 31, 2018.

Hernbroth, Megan, The era of the unicorn may be on its way out in 2020, Business Insider December 6, 2019.

Hirschauge, Orr and Deepa Seetharaman, Facebook Looks to Bring virtual Reality to Mobile Devices, The Wall Street Journal, July 29, 2015.

Hobson, Katherine, The case for a course of virtual reality, US News and World Report, September 4, 2019.

Hoffower, Hillary, More millennials are ditching big US cities for the suburbs and it shows just how dire the unaffordable housing crisis is, Business Insider, September 27, 2019.

Hoffower, Hillary, millennials are flooding into these 25 US cities to find good jobs and earn more money, Business Insider, December 23, 2019.

Holt, Kris, Google CEO Sundar Pichai Says AI Needs to Be Regulated, Forbes, January 20, 2020.

Huddleston, Cameron, Experts predict how long cash will survive, Go Banking Rates, January 24, 2019.

Hruska, Joel, Self-driving cars still can't handle snow, rain or heavy weather, Extreme Tech, October 30, 2018.

Javanmardian, Minoo, Lingampally, Aditya, Can AI Address Health Care's Red Tape Problem, Harvard Business Review, November 5, 2018.

Johnson, Eric, America desperately needs fiber internet, and the tech giants won't save us, Vox, January 10, 2019.

Johansson, Anna, The internet is due for a split, here's what you need to know, The Next Web, October 4, 2018.

Kapadia, Shefali, Trade and tech push supply chains from global to local, Supply Chain Drive, September 5, 2018.

Kapner, Suzanne, Data Pushes Aside Chief Merchants, The Wall Street Journal, September 20, 2015.

Khurana, Ryan, Artificial intelligence Needs Private Markets for Regulation – Here's Why, Observer, January 23, 2020.

Key Challenges in Big Data, Gartner, August 17, 2018.

Knight, Will, AI Is Biased. Here's How Scientists Are Trying to Fix It, Wired, December 19, 2019.

Kolodny, Lora, Former Google CEO predicts the internet will split in two – and one part will be led by China, CNBC, September 20, 2018.

Kusisto, Laura, Housing Market gaining modest strength, indicators show, Wall Street Journal, October 29, 2019.

Lloyd, Richard, The Rise of the Google Gorilla, Intellectual Asset Management Magazine November, 2015.

Laurie, Ron, Constructing a holistic corporate patent monetization strategy, Intellectual Asset Management Magazine, June, 2015.

Law Library of Congress: Regulation of Artificial Intelligence in selected Jurisdictions, The Law library of Congress global Research Directorate, January 2019.

Madrigal, Alexis, Waymo's Robots drove more miles than everyone else combined, The Atlantic, February 14, 2019.

Manyika, James, Silberg, Jake and Presten, Brittany, What do we do about the biases in AI?, Harvard Business Review, October 25, 2019.

Marshall, Jack, Apple Propels Cottage Industry of Ad Blockers, The Wall Street Journal, September 24, 2015.

Martin, Nicole, Okay Google, will voice be the future of search?, Forbes, November 6, 2018.

Marr, Bernard, The key definitions of artificial intelligence that explain its importance, Forbes, February 14, 2018.

Matte, Daniel and Mccullagh, Kevin, Will Smartwatches Be a Hit?, The Wall Street Journal, May 10, 2015.

McKenna, Michael, Three notable examples of AI Bias, AI Business, October 14, 2019.

McPharlin, Kelly, Why we should listen to Bill Gates on Nuclear Energy, NEI, February 4, 2019.

Meola, Andrew, What is the internet of things? What IO means and how it works, Business Insider, May 10, 2018.

Mire, Sam, What's the future of health care? 31 experts share their insights, Disruptor Daily, June 27, 2019.

MIT Technology Review; Asia's AI Agenda, The ethics of AI, 2019.

Morrison, Maureen, and Tim Peterson, The War on Advertising, Advertising Age, September 14, 2015.

Morrison, Maureen, The CMO's Guide to Messaging Apps, Advertising Age, September 14, 2015.

Morgan, Jacob, A simple explanation of the internet of things, Forbes, May 13, 2014.

Mui, Chunka & Carroll, Paul B, The New Killer Apps: How Large Companies Can Out-Innovate Start Ups, Cornerloft Press, 2013.

Nellis, Stephen, Dastin, Jeffrey, Microsoft wants to erase its carbon footprint – past and future, Reuters, January 17, 2020.

Nelson, Raymond, The future of fiber, Forbes, April 18, 2018.

Ngak, Chenda, As Google Fiber expands to Olathe, Kan., millions of Americans still offline, CBS News. 2013.

Nusca, Andrew, Net Neutrality Explain What It Means and Why It Matters, Fortune, November 23, 2017.

Oh, Soo Jin, Buyer Behavior Trends Driving the Digital Shift Toward Mobile, Marketing Land, June 17, 2015.

Oliver, Erik and Kent Richardson, The strategic counter-assertion model for patent portfolio RoI, Intellectual Asset Management Magazine, March 2015.

Oliver, Nick, Potocnik, Kristina and Calvard, Thomas, To Make Self Driving Cars Safe, We Also Need Better Roads and Infrastructure, Harvard Business Review, August 14, 2018.

Peterson, Tim, Entertainments engineers: How video is being reprogrammed at YouTube, Advertising Age, September 15, 2015.

Powell, Jessica, The Problem is Bigger Than We Work, Why wall street Realized Unicorns Aren't so Magical, Time Magazine, November 21, 2019.

Primack, Dan, Elizabeth Warren's trust-busting plan eyes Silicon Valley mergers, Axios, March 11, 2019.

Robot Technology, Encyclopedia Britannica, last updated November 27, 2019.

Rubin, Peter, Want to know the real future of AR/VR? Wired, August 5, 2019.

Seetharaman, Deepa, Oculus Adds Movies and TV, The Wall Street Journal, September 24, 2015.

Schmidt, Ann, Millennials are moving to these affordable cities, Fox Business, October 3, 2019.

Segan, Sascha, What Is 5G? PC, January 2, 2020.

Serwer, Andy with Zahn, Max, Why we should Celebrate the End of the Unicorn, Yahoo Finance, November 9, 2019.

Sharma, Amol and Shalini Ramachandran, HBO Explores the 'How' of Streaming Option, The Wall Street Journal, October 29, 2014.

Silberg, Jake, Manyika, Tackling bias in artificial intelligence and in humans, McKinsey Global Institute, June 2019.

Simon, Matt, What is a robot? Wired, August 24, 107.

Stamm, Stephanie, A Decade of Unicorns Ends With a Little Less Magic, Wall Street journal, December 17, 2019.

Stanford Encyclopedia of Philosophy, Artificial Intelligence, first published July 12, 2018

Stinson, Jim, Autonomous Trucking still Distant, Transport Topics, January 30, 2019.

Supply Chain Quarterly Staff, Supply chains shift from global to local, Supply Chain Quarterly, Q3 2018.

Taulli, Tom, How Bias Distorts AI, Forbes, August 4, 2019.

Tepper, Nona, Nearly two-thirds of B2B companies have mobile web sites and apps, Internet Retailer. July 31, 2015.

The Narrowing of the Open Web, Infographic Bloomberg Business Week October 28, 2019.

Topol, Eric, Your Smartphone Will See You Now, The Wall Street Journal, January 9, 2015.

Tree, an MIT Research Project, active from January 2017 to June 2017. www.media.mit.edu/projects/tree/overview/.

Verizon 2019 Data Breach Investigations Report.

Vincent, James, Alphabet CEO Sundar Pichai says there is no question that AI needs to be regulated, The Verge, January 20, 2020.

Vonck, Richard, Connecting with Our Connected World, The Futurist, World Future Society, 2013.

Varey, James, Wealthy Americans flee high tax states, take billions with them, Tax the rich, the rich leave, The Washington Times, April 10, 2019.

Wartzman, Rick, The Tricky Role of the CEO in a New Era of Social Responsibility, Wall Street Journal, December 12, 2019.

Webb, Amy how to Do Strategic Planning Like a Futurist, Future Today Institute July 30, 2019.

Wharton Knowledge, Why cash won't lose its cachet anytime soon, Knowledge @ Wharton, May 23, 2019.

With Big Data Comes Big Responsibility: An Interview with Alex 'Sandy' Pentland, Harvard Business Review, November 2014.

What will the future look like without net neutrality, WSJ Video, June 11, 2018. www.wsj.com/video/what-will-the-future-look-like-without-net-neutrality/A5A2F482-065B-4529-B495-921CBFF77FF9.html.

Wolfe, Jennifer, Blockchain in the Boardroom, Create Space, 2018.

World Economic Forum Community Paper, Transforming Infrastructure: Frameworks for Bringing the Fourth Industrial Revolution to Infrastructure, Davos 2020.

World Economic Forum Insight Report in Collaboration with Boston Consulting Group, The Net Zero Challenge: Fast Forward to Decisive Climate Action, January 2020.

World Economic Forum Insight Report in Collaboration with Marsh & McLennan and Zurich Insurance Group, The Global Risks Report 2020, January 2020.

World Economic Forum Insight Report in Collaboration with FIDO Alliance, Passwordless Authentication The next breakthrough in secure digital transformation, January 2020.

Yonck, Richard, Scenario: Life with the Internet of Everything, The Futurist, World Future Society, November – December 2013.

99 Firms.com, 36 Key Voice Search Statistics You Can No Longer Ignore, April 16, 2019.

Chapter 4

Basu, Eric, Target CEO Fired- Can You Be Fired If Your Company is Hacked?, Forbes, June 15 2014.

Beavers, Olivia, House Dem introduces bill requiring public firms to disclose cybersecurity expertise in leadership, The Hill, March 13, 2019.

Blue Coat, Do Not Enter: Blue Coat Research Maps the Web's Shadiest Neighborhoods, Blue Coat Systems, 2015.

Carr, Austin, Day, Matt, Frier, Sarah, and Gurman, Mark, "Yes, They're Listening", Bloomberg Business Week, December 16, 2019.

Cook, Tim, On Encryption, The Wall Street Journal. Dow & Jones Company, November 21, 2015.

Copeland, Jeff, Jack Jones and James Lam on NACD Blog: Get the right cybersecurity reports, Fair Institute, June 25, 2018.

CF Disclosure Guidance: Topic No. 2 Cybersecurity, Division of Corporation Finance Securities and Exchange Commission. October 13, 2011.

Cyber-security and Data Privacy Outlook and Review: 2013, Gibson, Dunn & Crutcher LLP, April 16, 2013.

Cybersecurity and the Board, Audit Committee Leadership Network in North America, Tapestry Networks. November 7, 2012.

Czarnecki, Gerald, Cyber Threats Necessitate A New Governance Model, NACD Directorship National Association of Corporate Directors, 2015.

Davidson, Gordon and Laura Finley, Cybersecurity and the Board, Stanford Directors College 2013. Fenwick & West LLP, 2013.

Deiss, Ryan, Customer Value Optimization: How to Build an Unstoppable Business, Digital Marketer, September 5, 2019.

Debouch, Jim, Board Perspective on Risk, Protiviti. 2015.

Dellinger, AJ, Understanding the First American Financial Data Leak: How did it happen and what does it mean? Forbes, May 26, 2019.

Deutscher, Stefan, Five Ways Business Directors Can Prepare for the Future of Cybersecurity, World Economy Forum, January 15, 2020.

Directors and IT: What Works Best: A user-friendly board Guide for Information Technology Oversight, Abridged Version. PricewaterhouseCoopers Center for Board Governance. 2012.

Dwoskin, Elizabeth, Data Privacy: Test Your Knowledge." The Wall Street Journal, April 29, 2015.

Dwoskin, Elizabeth, What is Encryption, Anyway?" The Wall Street Journal, April 29, 2015.

Epstein, Adam, Thinking Strategically About Cyber Risk, NACD Directorship. 2014.

Eadicicco, Lisa, A professional hacker reveals why so many companies are falling victim to data breaches, and the one thing every company should do to avoid getting hacked, Business Insider, November 11, 2019.

Gage, Deborah, VCs Pour Money Into Cybersecurity Startups, The Wall Street Journal, April 19, 2015.

Harding, Luke, How Edward Snowden went from loyal NSA contractor to whistleblower, The Guardian, February 1, 2014.

Hilk, Jeff and Jeffry Powell, Protecting Your Board Books, National Association of Corporate Directors, 2014.

Huang, Daniel, United They Stand, The Wall Street Journal, February 4, 2015.

Ikeda, Scott, Third Party Data Breaches Hits Quest Diagnostics with 12 million confidential patent records exposed, CPO Magazine, June 11, 2019.

Kokalitcheva, Kia, Fake Bloomberg news report drives Twitter Stock up 8%, Fortune, July 14, 2015.

Krebs on Security, May 24, 2019

Krawchenko, Katiana, The phishing email that hacked the account of John Podesta, October 28, 2016, CBS News.

Lee, Edmund, AP Twitter Account Hacked in Market-Moving Attack, Bloomberg Business, April 24, 2013.

Letter from Chairman Rockefeller to Chairman White on SEC Guidance, April 9 2013.

Loizos, Connie, Cybersecurity expert Alex Stamos on Facebook's counter-terrorism team and the private-public divide, TechCrunch, November 14, 2019.

Ma, Alexandra and Gilbert, Ben, Facebook understood how dangerous the trump linked data firm Cambridge Analytica could be much earlier than it previously said. Business Insider August 23, 2019.

MacAskill, Ewen, Edward Snowden, The Guardian, September 13, 2019.

Marchand, Ashley, Environmental and Competitive Disruptors Likely to Transform Board Agendas, National Association of Corporate Directors, September/October 2014.

McCoy, Kevin, Target to pay $18.5 million for 2013 data breach that affected 41 million consumers, USA today, May 23, 3017.

McLean, Rob, A Hacker gained access to 100 million capital one credit card applications and accounts, CNN Business, July 30, 2019.

McQuade, Mike, The Untold Story of NotPetya, The Most Devastating Cyber Attack in History, Wired, August 22, 2018.

Meeuwisse, Raef, How to get cybersecurity right in 2019, Info Security Magazine, January 16, 2019.

Meredith, Sam, Here's everything you need to know about the Cambridge Analytica scandal, CNBC, March 21, 2018.

Miller, Greg, The Snowden Files: The Inside Story of the World's Most Wanted Man, by Luke Harding, The Washington Post, February 14, 2014.

Monocraft, Bethan, State Farm Hit by data breach, Insurance Business Magazine, August 8, 2019.

Murnane, Kevin, How John Podesta's emails were hacked and how to prevent it from happening to you, Forbes, October 21, 2016.

NACD, Cyber-Risk Oversight: Director's Handbook Series, National Association of Corporate Directors 2014.

NACD, Questions for the Board to Ask Management about Cybersecurity, National Association of Corporate Directors, 2015.

NACD, Report for the 2015 NACD Blue Ribbon Commission: The Board and Long-Term Value Creation, National Association of Corporate Directors, 2015.

Neustar, April 2015 Neustar DDOS Attacks & Protection Report: North America, Neustar, Inc. 2015.

Orr, Jeff, State Farm Insurance discloses recent credential stuffing attack, Cybersecurity Hub, August 9, 2019.

Otto, Greg, What Capital One's cybersecurity team did and did not get right, CyberScoop, August 2, 2019,

Paletta, Damian, Cyberwar Ignites New Arms Race, The Wall Street Journal, October 11, 2015.

PC Magazine Encyclopedia, Deep Web Definition, PC Magazine.

Peregrine, Michael, Key board Takeaways from This Year's NACD Public Company Survey, Forbes, December 26, 2019,

Peterson, Hayley, Amazon engineer calls for Ring to be shut down immediately over privacy concerns, Business Insider, January 27, 2020.

PR Newswire, New Cybersecurity Governance Study Shows Dramatic Increase in Boards Addressing Cyber Risks, PR Newswire, October 2, 2015.

PwC, Cybersecurity is front and center, PwC, 2015.

PwC, Director confidence about cybersecurity, PwC, 2015.

PwC, IT strategy and IT risk mitigation, PwC, 2015.

PwC, Time spent on IT oversight, PwC, 2015.

PwC. Turnaround and transformation in cybersecurity: Key findings from The Global State of Information Security Survey 2016, PwC, 2015.

PwC. Where do directors want to spend more time?, PwC, 2015.

PwC. Who oversees IT risks? PwC, 2015.

Gordon, Davidson and Finley, Laura, Reading Materials for Board Members on Cybersecurity Attacks, Fenwick & West LLP, June 24, 2013.

Response Letter from Chairman White to Chairman Rockefeller on SEC Guidance, May 1, 2013.

Rowland, Christopher, Quest Diagnostics discloses breach of patient records, The Washington Post, June 3, 2019.

Samuel, Alexandra, The Weakest Security Link: Your Children, The Wall Street Journal, April 19, 2015.

Sandstrom, Thomas, Congress considered requiring public companies to disclose board member cybersecurity expertise in SEC filings, Georgetown Law Tech Review, June 2019.

Smith, Gerry, New York Post Confirms Twitter Accounts Were Hacked, Bloomberg Business. 2015.

Strategies to Mitigate Targeted Cyber Intrusions, Australian Government, Department of Defense, Cyber Security Operations Centre, October 2012.

Swarts, Angela, CEO heads may roll for security breaches in wake of Sony boss' exit, experts say, Silicon Valley Business Journal, February 9, 2015.

Truta, Filip, 60% of breaches in 2019 involved unpatched vulnerabilities, Security Boulevard, October 31, 2019.

Vijayan, Jaikumar, Target breach happened because of a basic network segmentation error, Computerworld, February 6, 2014.

Wallace, Gregory, HVAC vendor eyed as entry point for Target breach, CNN, February 6, 2014.

Weise, Elizabeth, Facebook's chief security officer Alex Stamos said to resign, USA Today, March 19, 2018.

Wemple, Erik, Bloomberg report of challenged big hack story gets promoted, The Washington Post, September 17, 2019.

White Paper: Protecting Against Web Application Threats Using SSL, Symantec Corporation, 2013.

Whittaker, Zack, Door dash confirms data breach affected 4.8 million customers, workers and merchants, TechCrunch, September 26, 2019.

Whittaker, Zack, Capital one replaces security chief after data breach, TechCrunch, November 7, 2019.

Wray, Christopher, Director of FBI, Worldwide Threats Statement before Senate Homeland security and Government Affairs, Washington D.C., November 5, 2019.

Yadron, Danny, Ashley Madison's Stolen Data Is Posted, The Wall Street Journal, August 19, 2015.

Yadron, Danny, The Man Who Finds the Security Holes, The Wall Street Journal, February 15, 2015.

Yadron, Danny, What Companies Should Be Doing to Protect Their Computer Systems- but Aren't, The Wall Street Journal, April 20, 2015.

Chapter 5

Akhtar, Allana, 13 six figure jobs for people who value stability and career growth, Business Insider, August 15, 2019.

Bethune, Sophie, Gen Z more likely to report mental health concerns, American Psychological Association, January 2019.

Bulajewski, Mike The sharing economy was dead on arrival, Daily Jestor, December 12, 2018.

Cox, Josie, The sharing economy is failing for one simple reason – people can't be trusted, The Independent, July 30, 2017.

Dillet, Romain What happened to the sharing economy? TechCrunch July 31, 2019.

Dimock, Michael, Defining generations: Where Millennials end and Gen Z begins, Pew Research Center, January 17, 2019.

Elmore, Tim, Generation Z Unfiltered: Facing Nine Hidden Challenges of the Most Anxious Population Poet Gardener Publishing, 2020.

Fain, Paul, Google Curriculum, College Credit, Inside Higher Ed, September 26, 2018.

Feuer, William, Airbnb reportedly lost money last year as costs ballooned ahead of its planned public listing this year, CNBC, February 11, 2020.

Florida, Richard, the changing demographics of America's suburbs, CityLab, November 7, 2019.

Franchises, Tracy, Hoefel, Fernanda, True Gen: Generation Z and its implications for companies, McKinsey and Company, 2020.

Garone, Elizabeth, Women Flock to Franchising, Wall Street Journal, December 1, 2019.

Generation Z is stressed, depressed and exam obsessed, The Economist, February 27, 2019.

Goldstein, Steve, why Uber and Lyft will fail miserably at autonomous driving, MarketWatch, August 30, 2019.

Groysberg, Boris, Lee, Jeremiah, Price, Jesse and Cheng, J. Yo-Jud, The Leaders Guide to Corporate Culture, Harvard Business Review, January/February 2018.

Hall, John, Why you should start considering universities for long term partnerships, Inc., March 17, 2019.

Isaac, Mike, Super Pumped the Battle for Uber, Lake Book 2019.

Jenkins, Ryan, This is the most in demand skill of the future, Inc. July 22, 2019.

Keil, Roger, Suburban change is transforming city life around the world, The Conversation, October 30, 2019.

Kiersz, Andy, These are the industries most likely to be taken over by robots, World Economic Forum, April 25, 2019.

Kinder, Molly, Putting the worker in the future of work, Brookings, November 19, 2019.

Kolczak, Amy, Five trends influencing the future of our cities, National Geographic, December 8, 2017.

Leighton, Heather, How suburbs are turning into hipsturbias to cater to millennials, Ric Kinder Institute for Urban Research, October 1, 2019.

Lutchen, Kenneth, Why companies and universities should form long term collaborations, Harvard Business Review, January 24, 2018.

Marr, Bernard, The 10 vital skills you will need for the future of work, Forbes, April 29, 2019.

Marr, Bernard, The Future of work: 5 Important Ways Jobs Will Change in the 4th industrial revolution. Forbes, July 15, 2019.

McBride, Stephen, Uber's nightmare has just begun, Forbes, September 4, 2019.

Muniz, Hanna, 17 best college majors for finding a job, Prep Scholar, October 22, 2019.

Palmer, Annie, Bosa, Deidre, Airbnb's quarterly loss reportedly doubled in Q1, a bad sign as investors grow wary of money losers, CNBC, October 17, 2019.

Paquette, Aaron, Gen Z Is poised to become the most entrepreneurial generation ever – even more so than millennials, Vision Critical, April 28, 2019.

Passy, Jacob Gen Z is financial better armed and better educated than millennials were at the same age, MarketWatch, January 29, 2020.

Patel, Deep, 8 Ways Generation Z will differ from millennials in the workplace, Forbes, September 21, 2017.

Penn, Joanna, Wighbey, John, Uber Airbnb and consequences of the sharing economy, Harvard Kennedy School, Journalists' Resource, June 3, 2016.

Preparing for the Future of Work, World Economic Forum, 2020.

Rapacon, Stacy, 25 best college majors for a lucrative career, Kiplinger, February 5, 2019.

Santana, Gisette, Millennials are flocking to the Suburbs, Rick Kinder Institute for Urban Research, June 5, 2017.

Schieber, Jonathan, Uber's losses top $1 billion, better than expected revenues, TechCrunch November 4, 2019.

Smith, Yves, Uber is headed for a crash, New York Magazine, December 4, 2018.

Spitznagel, Eric, Generation Z is bigger than millennials – and they're out to change the world, New York Post, January 25, 2020.

Staff reporter, Angie's List report first profitable year in company history, IBJ, February 23, 2016.

St Esprit, Meg, The stigma of choosing trade school over college, The Atlantic, March 6, 2019.

Thiefels, Jessica, 5 simple ways to assess company culture, Achievers, April 24, 2018.

Tomar, Dave, Trade schools on the rise: is trade school right for you? The Quad, January 9, 2020.

Walker, Alissa, A manifesto for a new suburbia, Curbed, November 11, 2019.

Wyckoff, Whitney Blair, The 25 best jobs of 2020, US News and World Report, January 7, 2020.

Zimmerman, Eli, Major companies partner with colleges for education opportunities in emerging tech, Ed Tech, July 10, 2018.

Chapter 6

Atkinson, Claire, Charlie Rose accused by 27 women of sexual harassment, NBC News, May 3, 2018.

Baker, Sinead, Davos says it is focusing on the climate crisis, but its billionaires and world leaders are still arriving on private jets, Business Insider, January 20, 2020.

Boitnott, John, Why your business should be more environmentally focused, according to recent climate change report, Inc., January 25, 2019.

Bouw, Brenda, Microsoft, Facebook, Other Tech Firms Face Workers' Climate Change Strike Friday, The Street, September 17, 2019.

Brown, Dalvin, Ex Google engineer who alleged discrimination against conservative white men asks judge to dismiss lawsuit, USA Today, May 10, 2020.

Chaykowski, Kathleen, Uber Whisteblower Susan Fowler on What Every Company Should Do To Stop Harassment, Forbes, April 10, 2018.

Corporate Board Member, How MeToo Is Reshaping Cultural Oversight, Corporate Board Member, April 5, 2018.

Creary, Stephanie, McDonnell, Mary-Hunter, Ghai, Sakshi, Scruggs, Jared, When and why diversity improves your board's performance, Harvard Business Review, March 27, 2019.

Desta, Yohana, Graphic, Disturbing details of Matt Lauer's alleged sexual misconduct, Vanity Fair, November 29, 2017.

Domonoske, Camila, After unsatisfying answers, United offers deepest apology for violent confrontation, NPR, April 11, 2017.

Ekin, Annette, Quotas get more women on boards and stir change from within, The EU Research and Innovation Magazine, September 6, 2018.

Ellesser, California Mandates Women on Corporate Boards, But do quotas work? Forbes, October 2, 2018.

Flanagan, Caitlin, Matt Lauer's Woman Problem, The Atlantic, November 5, 2019.

Frehse, Rob, Charlie Rose sued for sexual harassment by former makeup artist, CNN, September 21, 2019.

Frick, Walter, Study: Green advertising helped BP recover from the deep water horizon spill, Harvard Business Review, February 5, 2014.

Garcia, Anthony, Direct skills: Diversity of Thought and Experience in the Boardroom, ISS, October 10, 2018.

Gold, Russell, Microsoft strives for a carbon free future. A setback in Fargo shows the hard reality. Wall Street Journal, January 30, 2020.

Green, Alison, Can your employer forbid you from talking politics at work?, US News and World Report, March 14, 2016.

Hartmans, Avery, The engineer who blew the whistle on Uber's culture of sexual harassment was just hired by the New York times, Business Insider, July 23, 2018.

Helsel, Phil, Matt Lauer accused of raping NCB colleague, Ronan Farrow book alleges, NBC, October 9, 2019.

Hinds, Rebecca Hinds, This is what makes these CEOs on Twitter Brilliant, Inc., January 18, 2019.

Hopkins, Anna, Judge rules lawsuit accusing Google of bias against conservatives can proceed, Fox News, June 10, 2019.

Hyken, Shep, Starbucks Closes 8,000 Stores for Racial bias Training – Is It Enough, Forbes, June 1, 2018.

James, Meg, CBS' Leslie Moonves sex scandal: Portrait emerges for a culture of fear, entitlement – and little accountability, Los Angeles Times, December 9, 2018.

Kell, George, The remarkable rise of ESG, Forbes, July 11, 2018.

Koop, Fermin, Growing demand for private jets challenge climate action, ZME Science, October 29, 2019.

Knight, Rebecca, Should you talk about politics at work? Harvard Business Review, September 26, 2016.

Kramer, Mark, The backlash to Larry Fink's letter shows how far business has to go on social responsibility, Harvard Business Review, January 31, 2019.

Leskin, Paige, From Elon Musk to Bill Gates, here are all of the notable tech billionaires who jet around the world in private planes, Business Insider, June 17, 2019.

Levin, Bess, United CEO offers the worst possible response to the airline's PR disaster, Vanity Fair, April 11, 2017.

Lyons, Erin, It's time for the ad industry to address climate change, Marketing Week, Mary 29, 2019.

Massa, Annie, BlackRock CEO Larry Fink puts climate change at center of megafund's investment strategy, Fortune, January 14, 2020.

Meyer, Russ, A history of green brands: 1980s green shoots appear, Fast Company, May 13, 2010.

Mounk, Yascha, Americans strongly dislike PC culture, The Atlantic, October 10, 2018.

Montanaro, Domenico, Warning to democrats: most Americans against US getting more politically correct, NPR, All things considered, December 19, 2008.

Mulcahy, Emma, When brands go green: how sustainability and environmentalism shape marketing campaigns, The Drum, June 14, 2019.

National Association of Corporate Directors Public Company Governance Survey, 2019-2020.

Pontefract, Dan, Decoding BlackRock chairman Larry Fink's letter to CEOs on the importance of purpose, Forbes, January 26, 2019.

Person, Thad, Should you talk politics at work? Monster.com.

Segarra, Lisa Marie, More than 20,00 google employees participated in walkout over sexual harassment policy, Fortune, November 3, 2018.

S&P Global Ratings, Environmental, Social and Governance Evaluation Analytical Approach, April 10, 2019.

Solovieva, Daria, One year later: #metoo movement enters the boardroom, The Street, October 9, 2018.

Stych, Anne, Women's representation on boards reaches milestone, Biz Women Journals, September 12, 2019.

Stych, Anne, Forbes faces backlash after only one woman makes innovators list, Bizwomen Journals, September 10, 2019.

The Guardian, the troubling evolution of corporate greenwashing, August 20, 2016.

Tung, Liam, Google employee protest: Now Google backs off Pentagon drone AI project, ZDNet June 4, 2018.

White, Martha, #Metoo in the boardroom: it takes more than a symbolic gesture to change corporate culture, NBC January 11, 2018.

Chapter 7

Allianz, Digital Agenda, June 2019.

Atkins, Betsy, Corporate Governance in 2020, Forbes, January 9, 2020.

Cloyd, Mary Ann, Taking a Fresh Look at Board Composition, PricewaterhouseCoopers LLP, 2013.

Deloitte Insights, Tech Trends 2020.

Does Going Public Affect Innovation?, Shai Bernstein Stanford Graduate School of Business Research Paper Series, Research Paper No. 212, December 2012.

Gallagher, Ryan, Google employees uncover ongoing work on censored China search, The Intercept, March 4, 2019.

Hubbard, Douglas W, How to Measure Anything: Finding the Value of Intangibles in Business, John Wiley & Sons, 2007.

Hurd, D'Anne, Vitale, Mary Beth, The Board's Operating Model, National Association of Corporate Directors, Director Professionalism, March 2020.

Huskins, Priya Cherian, Woodruff Sawyer Management Liability D&O Insights: 2020 D&O Insurance Trends: A Look Ahead Guide, September 10, 2019.

McKinsey & Company, The Board Perspective: A Collection of McKinsey insights focusing on boards of directors, August 2016.

Meixler, Eli, Here's why google employees are protecting the company's planned expansion in China, Time, November 28, 2018.

National Association of Corporate Directors, Adaptive Governance: Board Oversight of Disruptive Risks, 2018.

National Association of Corporate Directors, 2020 Governance Outlook, Projections on Emerging Board Matters, 2019.

National Association of Corporate Directors Public Company Governance Survey 2019-2020.

National Association of Corporate Directors Blue Ribbon Commission on Culture as a Corporate Asset, 2017.

New California Law Mandates Female Representation on Board of Directors by December 2019, The National Law Review, February 17, 2020

Peniston, Bradley, Google's withdrawal from pentagon AI project risks U.S. lives, Defense One, June 26, 2018.

Peregrine, Michael, The boards, they are a transformin' Forbes, November 6, 2019.

PC360 Staff Writer, D&O coverage insights for organizations in 2020, Property Casualty 360, January 16, 2020.

PwC, Governing for the long term: Looking down the road with an eye on the rear –view mirror, PwC. 2015.

Sidley Best Practices Calendar for Corporate Boards and Committees 2019, Sidley Austin, LLP.

Solis, Brian, What's the Future of Business? Changing the Way Businesses Create Experiences, John Wiley & Sons, 2013.

Stanford Business Rock Center for Corporate Governance, 2106 Board of Directors Evaluation and Effectiveness.

Woodruff Sawyer, Looking Ahead 2020, D&O Considerations, 2020.

Zillman, Claire, The EU is taking a drastic step to put more women on corporate boards, Fortune, November 20, 2018.

Index

A

Agenda reboot, 152
Agriculture science, 95
Airbnb, 14
Alexa voice-based search, 22
Amazon, 3, 5, 22
Amazon Web Services (AWS), 52
Annual calendar, 140, 141
Anthropological approach of culture, 102, 103
Artificial intelligence (AI), 9, 30, 40, 90, 161
Audit, 133
Augmented reality, 41
Automation, 88–90
Automation meets infrastructure, 43

B

Bell Labs, 2
The Big Hack, 55
Biometrics, 46
Bitcoin, 45
Blockbuster, 6, 20, 21
Blockchain, 42
Board evaluations, 141, 153, 155, 156
Board members, 122
Board of directors, 46
Board refreshment and
    composition, 126–129

Boardroom
    agenda reboot, 152
    board calendar, events, 153
    board composition, 152
    board evaluations, 153, 155, 156
    building environment, 125
    calendar planning, best practices, 140–143
    committees and traditional board
        agenda, 130
    committee structure reboot, 152
    disruptive trends
        directors and officers liability and
            insurance, 149, 150
        industry best practices, 150, 151
        Legislation/SEC, 148, 149
    effectively present information, 146
    general principles, 156
    individual board members
        activity, 143, 144
    new skills matrix, 151
    right people, 126–129
Boeing, 9, 10
Business of health care, 44
Business practices, 4

C

Cameras, 70
Capital One, 52, 71
Climate change, 43, 110, 111
Committees
    audit, 133
    compensation and culture, 135, 136

J. C. Wolfe, *Disruption in the Boardroom*, https://doi.org/10.1007/978-1-4842-6159-0

Committees (*cont.*)
    nominating and Governance, 134, 135
    risk, 136, 137
    and traditional board agenda, 130
Competitive analytics, 143
Competitors, 25
Compliance, 94
Consumer goods, 46
Continuous learning, 29, 93
2020 Coronavirus Pandemic, 21, 33, 36, 38,
        42, 46, 86, 122
Corporate communities, 37
Corporate governance, 121
Corporate social responsibility, 108
Crisis and business continuity, 125
Crisis readiness, 142
CrowdStrike, 72
Cultural assessment
    anthropological approach, 102, 103
    proprietary methods, 102
    self-assessment, 103, 104
Cultural shifts, 92
Culture and incentives, 124
Culture assessment, 142
Cyber breaches, breakdown, 57
Cybersecurity, 45, 148
    annual risk appetite and cost-benefit
        analysis, 58
    best practices, experts, 71
    breaches occur, 63, 64
    Capital One, 52
    companies getting it right, 71
    company might be targeted, 62, 63
    2020 Coronavirus Pandemic, 52
    DoorDash, 54
    "Enron" moment, 51
    exposure points
        IT infrastructure, 58
        people (see "People" exposure point,
            cybersecurity)
        physical and digital entry and
            security, 58
    Facebook, 54
    framework, discussion and decision
        making, 72–80

legislation, 67–70
NotPetya, 56
questions to ask
    crisis communication preparedness, 66
    internet of things (IoT) lockdown, 67
    malware, phishing, inside jobs, 66
    open source compliance, 65
    personal devices, 67
    privacy compliance, 65
    ransomware preparedness, 66
    readiness for artificial
        intelligence (AI), 66
    trust but verify, 67
responsibilities, 56–58
risk accountability, 78
risk assessment, 79
State Farm, 53

D

Data clouds, 51
Data privacy, 39
Demand-driven learning grows, 91
Digital currency, 45
Digital mapping framework, 145, 146
Digital mapping of disruptive risks, 141
Digital technology, 24
Digital trends
    AI and robotics, 40
    automation meets infrastructure, 43
    biometrics, 46
    cybersecurity, 45
    digital currency, 45
    driverless cars, 34, 35
    drones, 32, 33
    5G, fiber optic, and speed, 37, 38
    global internet decentralization, 38, 39
    health care, 44
    housing market, 36, 37
    new energy sources, 35, 36
    supply chain, 43
    supply chains and management, 42
    tech trust busting and data privacy, 39
    virtual and augmented reality, 41
    voice-based search, 30, 32
Directors, 122, 149, 150
Disrupted boardroom, calendar planning,
        140–143

Disruption, 21, 22

Disruptive trends, 30

Diversity, 113, 114

DoorDash, 54

Dot-com bubble burst, 5

Driverless cars, 34, 35

Drone innovators network, 33

Drone technology, 32, 33

E

Earning extra money, 97

Ecommerce platform, 21, 22

Effective executive, 25

Employment agreements, 73

Energy sources, 35, 36

Enterprise risk, 124, 141

Entitlement generation, 85

Environmental and social, 125

Environmental and social governance (ESG)
    diversity, 113, 114
    environmental issues and climate change,
        110, 111
    leadership in digital age, 109
    #MeToo and sexual harassment, 112, 113
    political polarization and activism, 115, 116
    stakeholder values, 107

Environmental issues, 110, 111

Equifax, 8, 9, 55

F

Facebook, 5, 54

Factor Analysis of Information Risk (FAIR)
    Institute, 72

Fiber optic, 37

Financial accountability, 123

Financial Accounting Standards Board
    (FASB), 148

Firms, 72

First American Financial, 53

5G, 37

Future board skills matrix, 129

G

Gender and racial diversity, 115

General Data Protection
    Regulation (GDPR), 38

General Magic, 10

Generation Z, 86–88

Global internet decentralization, 38, 39

Google, 3, 5

Governance and compliance, 123, 124

H

Health care and wellness, 95

Housing market, 36, 37

Human Resources (HR), 61, 89

I

Incentives, 20, 21

Independence, 124

Individual board member activity, 143, 144

Industry best practices, 150, 151

Inside jobs, 60, 61

Intellectual honesty, 1

Interconnectedness, 47

Internal research and development (R&D), 99

Internet of Things (IoT), 43, 162

Internet service providers (ISPs), 37

Inventor, 24

J

Judgment, ethics, and decision making, 94

K

Kodak, 6, 21

L

Leadership in digital age, 109

Legacy practices, 137

Legacy structure of boards, 123

Legislation, cybersecurity, 67–70

M

Management presentations via webinar, 142

Mental health, 96, 97

Mergers and acquisitions, 48, 125

#MeToo, 112, 113

Millennial approach, 84, 85

Moral courage, 19

N

National Association of Corporate Directors (NACD), 2

Nest cameras, 39

Netflix, 5

"New Rule" business models, 5
    best practices, 4
    outcome health, 14
    Theranos, 11, 12
    Uber, 13, 14
    WeWork's, 12, 13
    Yahoo!, 15

NotPetya, 56

O

Officers, 149

Old rule–driven companies
    Blockbuster, 6
    Boeing, 9, 10
    Equifax, 8, 9
    General Magic, 10
    Kodak, 6
    Wells Fargo, 7, 8

Open source compliance, 65

Oversight, 94

P

Partnerships and strategic alignments, 47

Patent analytics, 25

Patents, 24

"People" exposure point, cybersecurity
    inside jobs, 60, 61
    phishing, 59, 60
    trust but verify information provided internally, 61, 62

Phishing, 59, 60, 72

Political correctness, 108

Political polarization and activism, 115, 116

Privacy, 70, 94

Privacy compliance, 65

Programming and patching vulnerabilities, 94

Proprietary culture assessments, 102

Psychological services, 96

Public Company Accounting Oversight Board (PCAOB), 148

Q

Quest Diagnostics, 53

R

Refreshed board agenda, 137–139

Resident-driven communities, 37

Return to locally *vs.* globally sourced, 43

Ring cameras, 39

Risk accountability, 78

Risk and compensation/culture committee, 144

Risk assessment, 79

Robotics, 40, 88–90, 162

Rules, 3, 4

S

Sales as a profession, 93

Securities and Exchange Commission (SEC), 45

Security, 94, 124

Self-assessment of culture, 103, 104

Senior management, 146

Sexual harassment, 112, 113

Sharing economy, 97, 98

Skill building, workforce, 91, 92

Social media, 3, 109

Social media monitoring, 73

Societal shifts, 101

Speed, 37

Stakeholder engagement assessment, 116–118

Stakeholders, 137

State Farm, 53

Status quo
  culture, 21, 23–25
  leadership, 25
  moral courage, 25
  patent portfolio, 24
  plan, board meeting, 26
  problem of managing, 20
  silo mentality, 20
  thinking and silo mentalities, 20

Subject matter expert groups, 123

Succession planning, 123

Supply chain, 42, 43, 47

T

Talent pipeline, 143

Tech trust busting, 39

TerraPower, 36

Theranos, 11, 12

Traditional board agenda, 131, 132

Traditional board calendar, 132, 133

Trust but verify, 143

Twitter, 5

U

Uber, 13, 14

Unicorns, 42

US Securities and Exchange Commission
  (SEC), 148, 149

V

Virtual reality, 41

Voice-based search, 30, 32

Voice recognition software, 32

W, X

Wells Fargo, 7, 8

WeWork's, 12, 13

Wireless nodes, 51

Workforce
  American Dream 2.0, 98, 99
  automation, 88
  cultural assessment (see Cultural
    assessment)
  diversity, 114
  educating and skill building, 90–92
  generations, 84
  Generation Z, 86–88
  issue and opportunity, 89
  mental health, 96, 97
  Millennial approach, 84, 85
  own businesses, 98
  robots, 88, 90
  rural areas, 99–101
  sharing economy, 97, 98
  skills
    agriculture science, 95
    construction and development, 95
    continuous learning, 93
    creativity and innovation, 93
    energy, space, and engineering, 95
    experience society, 92
    health care and wellness, 95
    Human Resources and human
      capital, 94
    judgment, ethics, and decision
      making, 94
    oversight, security, compliance, and
      privacy, 94
    programming and patching
      vulnerabilities, 94
    psychological support and human
      coaching, 95
    sales as a profession, 93
  suburban areas, 100, 101
  urban areas, 99–101

Workplace
  diversity, 113, 114
  political polarization and activism, 115, 116

Y

Yahoo, 15

Z

Zero-tolerance approach, 112

Zoom meetings, 39

CPSIA information can be obtained
at www.ICGtesting.com
Printed in the USA
LVHW021701020920
664876LV00005B/138

9 781484 261583